AUSTRALIAN

Signpost

MATHS

Mentals 2

Alan McSeveny Rachel McSeveny Diane McSeveny-Foster

Pearson Australia
(a division of Pearson Australia Group Pty Ltd)
459–471 Church St, Level 1, Building B, Richmond, Victoria, 3121
PO Box 23360, Melbourne, Victoria 8012
www.pearson.com.au

First published 2024 by Pearson Australia
2028 2027 2026 2025
10 9 8 7 6 5 4 3 2 1

Publishers: Sophie Matta and Kerry Nagle
Project Manager: Michelle Thomas
Production Editor: Laura Rentsch
Structural Editor: Rachel Elliott
Designer: Anne Donald
Typesetter: Integra
Proofreader: Ann M. Philpott
Rights & Permissions Editor: Alice McBroom
Cover Art: Michael Barter
Illustrator: Michael Barter
Publishing Services Analyst: Jit-Pin Chong
Printed in Malaysia by Vivar

ISBN 978 0 6557 0882 7

Pearson Australia Group Pty Ltd ABN 40 004 245 943

Acknowledgement of Country
Pearson respects and honours Aboriginal and Torres Strait Islander Elders past, present and future. We acknowledge the stories, traditions and living cultures of the Traditional Custodians of the lands on which our company is located and where we conduct our business. Pearson is committed to honouring Australian Aboriginal and Torres Strait Islander peoples' unique cultural and spiritual relationships to the land, waters and seas and their rich contribution to society.

Aboriginal and Torres Strait Islander peoples are advised that this text may contain images, voices and names of deceased persons.

Attributions
Pearson India Education Services Pvt. Ltd: Charadva, Sanjay, p. 67 (bee).
Shutterstock: agung wijayanto, ahmad, p. 64 (mask); Angel Salinas Salinas, Miguel, p. 63 (soup cans); Gaidamashchuk, p. 66 (baseball); Gerasimoski, Dragana, p. 64 (nail); mochi2001, p. 63 (submarine); Mujiono, Teguh, p. 59 (elephant).

Introduction

Using the Mentals Books

Each unit of a Mentals Book is programmed to review content from the previous two units of the Student Books. For example, Signpost Mentals Book Unit 5 can be used to review Signpost Student Book Units 3 and 4 while the Student Book Unit 5 is being taught. Unit 5 from both books should be completed in the same week.

Presentation

- The content of the strands Number, Algebra, Measurement, Space, and Statistics is revised.
- Essential number skills and language are given a high profile.

ID cards

- The ID cards on pages 5 and 6 review important terms addressed at Year 2 level.
- These cards can be used over and over again to improve and consolidate understanding.

Mixed-topic questions

The units present questions in a mixed-topic format.

- This is essential for thorough understanding and continuous review.
- It will allow the teacher to discover weaknesses that could otherwise pass unnoticed.
- The approach reflects real life – similar questions do not often occur together.
- It provides a real test of understanding.

If you do not use a Student Book

This book will be invaluable to those who do not use a Student Book, as it ensures both thorough coverage and constant review of the syllabus content.

Multiple-choice questions

The multiple-choice questions on page 78 introduce a variety of question types.

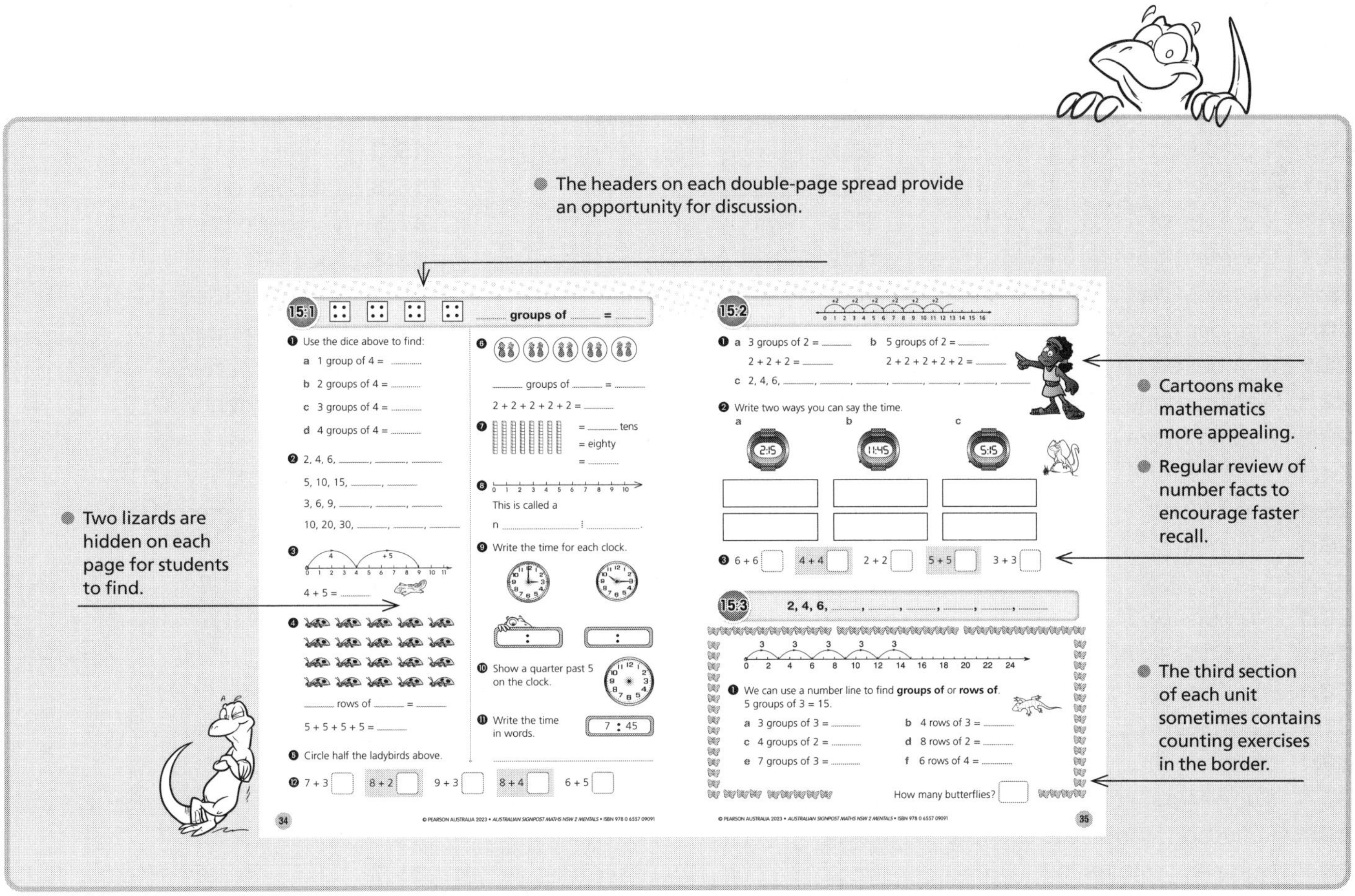

1 Contents

Unit header activities

1:1	8 – 2 (Q3)	**1:2**	9 – 4	**1:3**	7 + 4
2:1	10 + 2 (Q5, 7)	**2:2**	How many suns? (Q1)	**2:3**	9 – 3 (Q1)
3:1	6 + 4 (Q7)	**3:2**	How many boats? (Q1)	**3:3**	5 + 4
4:1	5 + 4 (Q2)	**4:2**	8 + 3	**4:3**	9 + 6 + 3
5:1	2D shapes (Q3, 7)	**5:2**	Months of the year (Q2)	**5:3**	Number patterns (Q1)
6:1	Days in each month (Q6)	**6:2**	7 – 3 (Q1)	**6:3**	10 + 2 (Q1)
7:1	Analog times (Q1)	**7:2**	2 groups of 3 (Q1)	**7:3**	10 + 6
8:1	2D shapes (Q5, 6)	**8:2**	2D shapes (Q1)	**8:3**	3 groups of 3 (Q1)
9:1	Number line (Q1, 5)	**9:2**	3 groups of 3 (Q2)	**9:3**	2D shapes
10:1	Number line (Q1, 5)	**10:2**	8 – 2 (Q2)	**10:3**	8 – 5 (Q1)
11:1	Number pattern (Q7, 8)	**11:2**	7 + 3 (Q4)	**11:3**	Number pattern
12:1	Number pattern (Q2, 7)	**12:2**	9 – 3 (Q2)	**12:3**	Number pattern
13:1	Tally marks	**13:2**	Number pattern	**13:3**	Number pattern
14:1	5 groups of 3 (Q2, 6, 9)	**14:2**	4 groups of 5 (Q1)	**14:3**	5 groups of 2 (Q1)
15:1	4 groups of 4 (Q2, 6, 8)	**15:2**	Number line pattern (Q1)	**15:3**	Number pattern (Q1)
16:1	4 groups of 6 (Q1, 4, 8, 12)	**16:2**	10 – 3	**16:3**	4 groups of 3
17:1	3 groups of 4 (Q1, 2, 6)	**17:2**	6 groups of 1	**17:3**	Number pattern
18:1	Counting from 200	**18:2**	10 + 10 (Q1)	**18:3**	3 x 8
19:1	Number line pattern	**19:2**	Coins (Q1)	**19:3**	Number pattern (Q1)
20:1	Number pattern (Q7)	**20:2**	Number pattern	**20:3**	Number pattern
21:1	Number pattern	**21:2**	Area	**21:3**	Number pattern
22:1	Adding money (Q8, 9, 12)	**22:2**	Area (Q2)	**22:3**	Adding money (Q1)
23:1	Adding money (Q8, 9)	**23:2**	Adding money (Q1)	**23:3**	3 groups of 2
24:1	3 groups of 2	**24:2**	3D objects (Q4)	**24:3**	Adding money (Q1)
25:1	6 + 7 (Q10)	**25:2**	Number pattern	**25:3**	Number pattern
26:1	Tally marks	**26:2**	Counting from 145	**26:3**	Number pattern (Q1)
27:1	12 ÷ 2 (Q2)	**27:2**	3 groups of 4	**27:3**	2 groups of 8
28:1	3 groups of 3	**28:2**	4 groups of 2	**28:3**	Adding 9 (Q1)
29:1	Counting from 127	**29:2**	How many eagles?	**29:3**	Number bonds
30:1	Months / seasons (Q6, 7)	**30:2**	3 groups of 4	**30:3**	Tally marks
31:1	2D shapes (Q6, 7)	**31:2**	Number pattern	**31:3**	Ordinal numbers (Q1)
32:1	Doubling (Q2, 3, 4, 9)	**32:2**	Months of the year (Q1)	**32:3**	Doubling (Q1)
33:1	Number pattern (Q8)	**33:2**	Number pattern (Q3)	**33:3**	2 groups of 3
34:1	Reflection, turn, slide (Q6)	**34:2**	3D objects (Q1)	**34:3**	Number bonds
35:1	Number combinations (Q6)	**35:2**	3D objects (Q1)	**35:3**	Number patterns (Q1)

ID card A

Do not write on this card.

ID card A

1

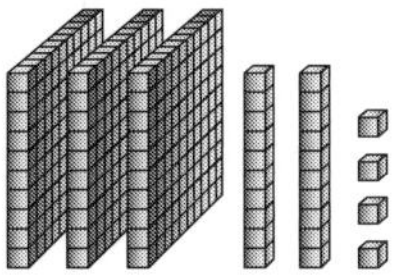

place-value

b________

2

n________ expander

3

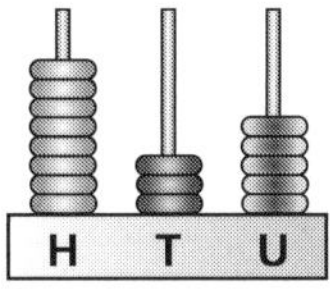

a________

4

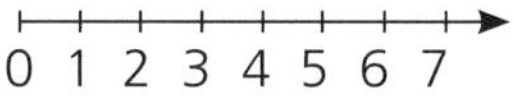

is a number

l________

5

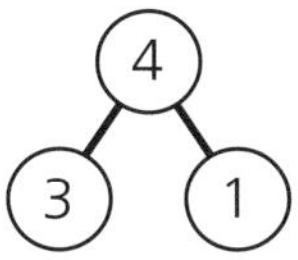

n________

b________

6

+

a________ or

p________

7

−

t______ a______,

s________

or m________

8

X

m________

sign

9

÷

d________

sign

10

=

is e________ to

11

24 + 9 = 33

is a number

s________

12

20th, 21st, 22nd

are

o________

numbers

13

2, 4, 6, 8...

are

e________

numbers

14

1, 3, 5, 7...

are

o________

numbers

15

m________

16

$

means ________

17

c

means ________

18

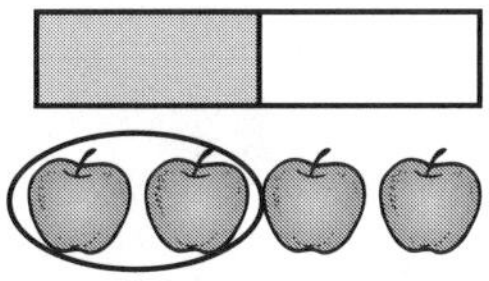

one h________

19

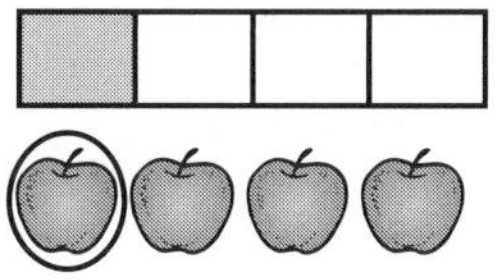

one q________

20

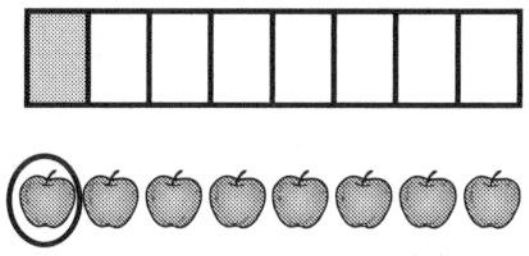

one e________

21

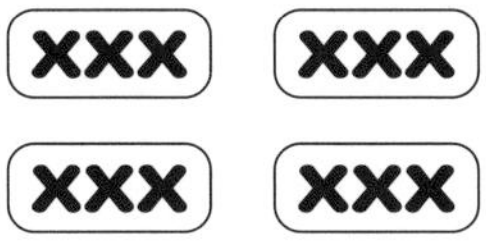

g________ of

22

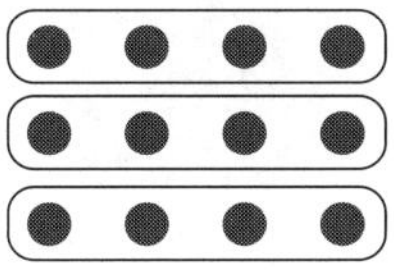

r________ of

23

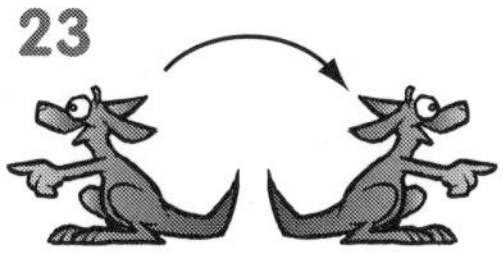

r________ or

f________

24

s________

25

t________

26

l________ hand

27

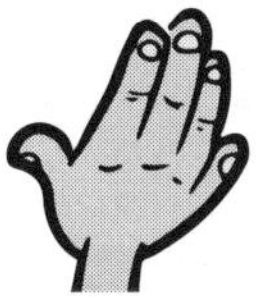

r________ hand

28

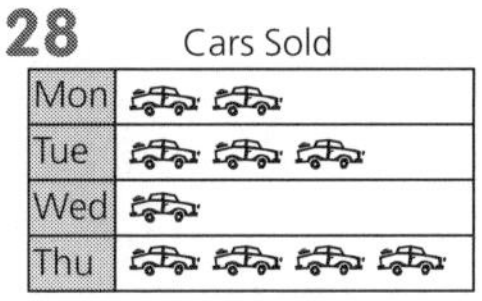

p________

graph

29

Birds	7
Lions	4
Monkeys	5

t________

30

t________

See page A1 for answers.

ID card B

Do not write on this card.

1

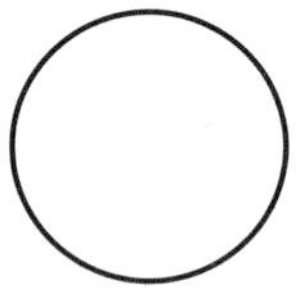

c____________

2

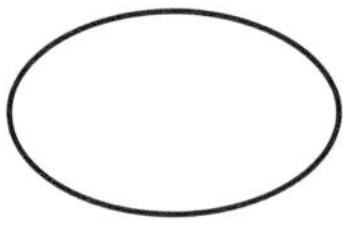

o____________

3

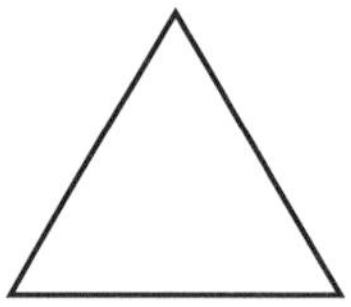

t____________

4

s____________

5

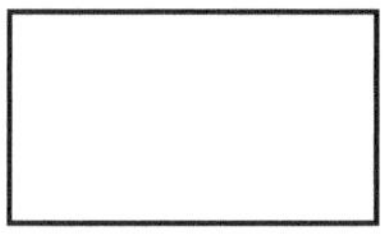

r____________

6

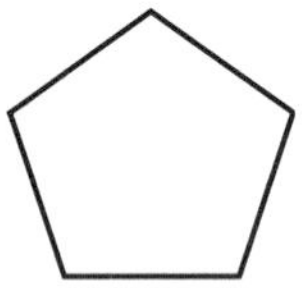

p____________

7

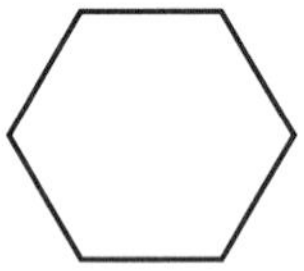

h____________

8

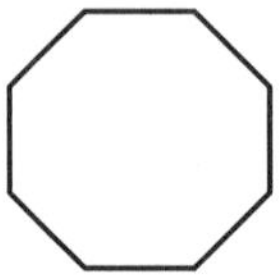

o____________

9

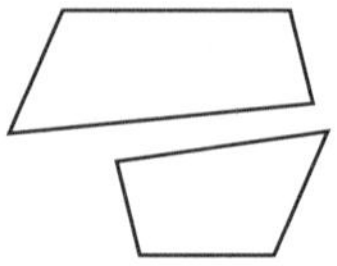

q____________

10

p__________ lines

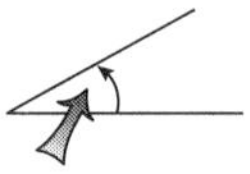

a____________

11

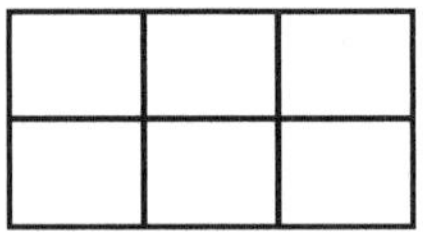

area is

_________ squares

12

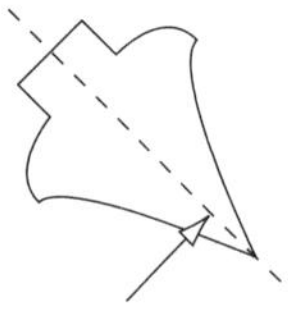

line of

s____________

13

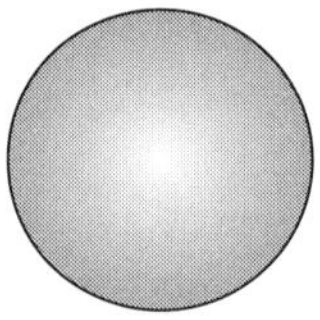

s____________

14

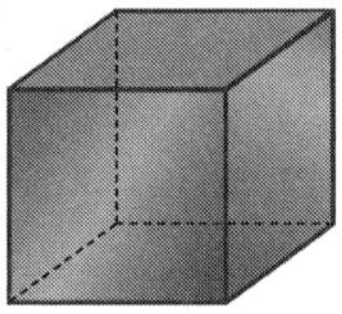

c____________

15

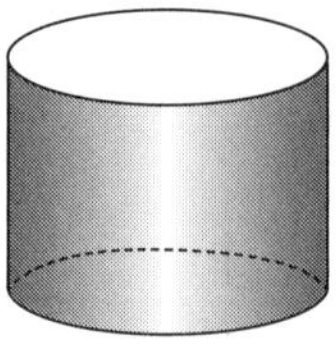

c____________

16

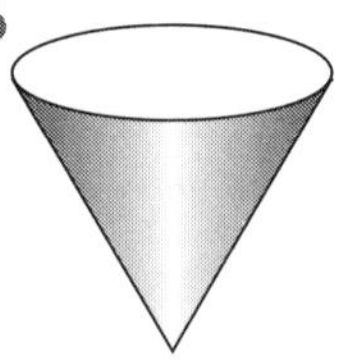

c____________

17

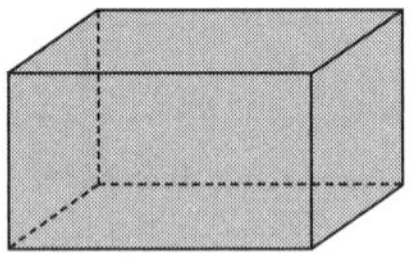

p____________

18

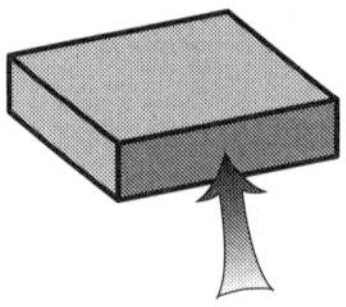

f__________

19

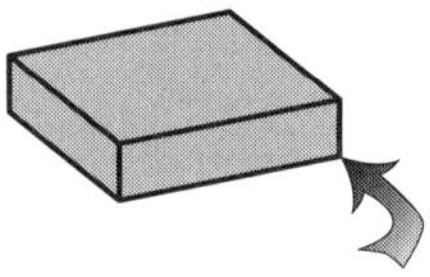

v__________

(or corner)

20

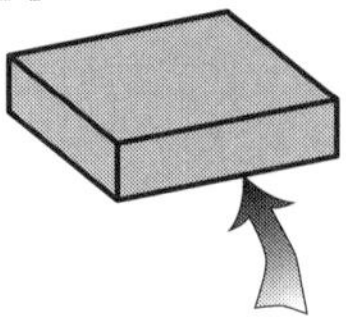

e__________

21

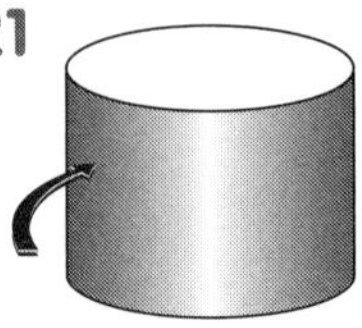

c____________

surface

22

f____________

surface

23

a____________

clock

24

d____________

clock

25

________ o'clock

26

half past ________

27

quarter past ______

28

quarter to _______

29

February

S	M	T	W	T	F	S
		1	2	3	4	5
6	7	8	9	10	11	12
13	14	15	16	17	18	19
20	21	22	23	24	25	26
27	28					

c____________

30

b____________

scales

See page A1 for answers.

 ISBN 978 0 6557 0882 7

Lizards

How would you name each lizard? Find two lizards on each page of this book.

1

2

3

4

5

6

7

8

9

10

11

12

13

14

Real names:

1 Horned lizard **2–3** Bearded dragon **4** Gecko **5** Shingleback lizard
6–11 Common garden lizard **12** Blue-tongue lizard **13** Skink
14 Frilled-neck lizard

1:1

❶ What number comes before:

a 6? ______ **b** 13? ______

❷ Write the total for each domino.

______ ______ ______ ______

❸

10 – 4 = ______

❹ Write the numeral for:

a fifteen ______

b ten ______

c twelve ______

d three ______

e nineteen ______

❺

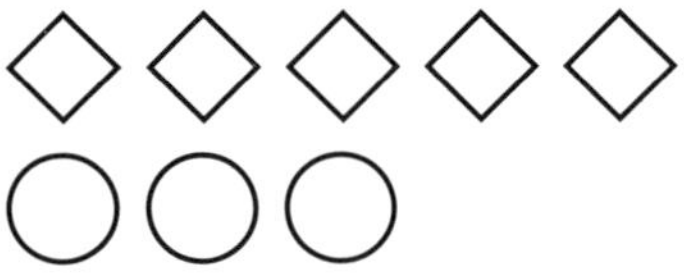

How many more squares are there? ______

5 – 3 = ______

❻ Fill in the missing numbers.

______ + ______ = ______

❼ **a** Share 12 circles among 2 boxes.

One share = ______ circles

b Share 16 squares among 2 boxes. One share = ______ squares

❽ How many dots?

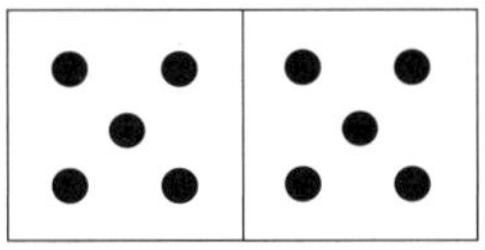

______ + ______ = ______

❾ How many days in one week? ______

❿ 8 take away 5. ______

9 minus 3. ______

7 plus 6. ______

6 take away 4. ______

⓫ 2 + 2 ☐ 4 + 1 ☐ 4 + 2 ☐ 3 + 2 ☐ 5 + 2 ☐

 ISBN 978 0 6557 0882 7

1:2

9 - 4 = ☐

❶ **a** Match these analog clocks with the correct time below.

4 o'clock   10 o'clock   2 o'clock   7 o'clock

b What number does the minute hand point to when the time is 9 o'clock? ☐

❷ Draw each shape using the lines on this grid.

square   pentagon   hexagon   octagon

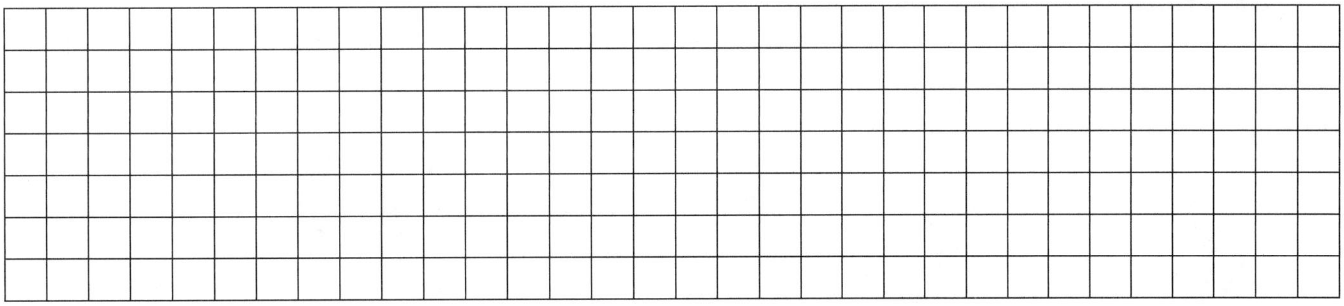

❸ 3 + 3 ☐   5 + 4 ☐   3 + 4 ☐   4 + 4 ☐   5 + 5 ☐

1:3

☐ + ☐ = ☐

1	2	3	4	5		7	8	9	10
11	12	13		15		17	18	19	
		23	24		26		28	29	30
	32		34	35	36	37	38	39	40
41	42	43	44		46	47		49	

❶ What is the number after:

26? ______   49? ______

❷ What is the number before:

32? ______   21? ______

❸ Complete the table.

 • *AUSTRALIAN SIGNPOST MATHS 2 MENTALS* • ISBN 978 0 6557 0882 7

+
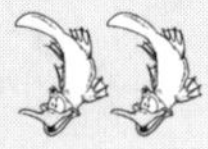

☐ + ☐ = ☐

❶
3	4	2	2
+ 2	+ 5	+ 2	+ 7
☐	☐	☐	☐

❷
8	9	7	10
– 2	– 4	– 4	– 5
☐	☐	☐	☐

❸ Write the total for each domino.

______ ______ ______

❹

Circle: The girl is on the **left** / **right** of the pony.

❺

______ + ______ = ______

❻ 9 minus 2. ______

7 take away 3. ______

4 plus 6. ______

❼ How many balloons?

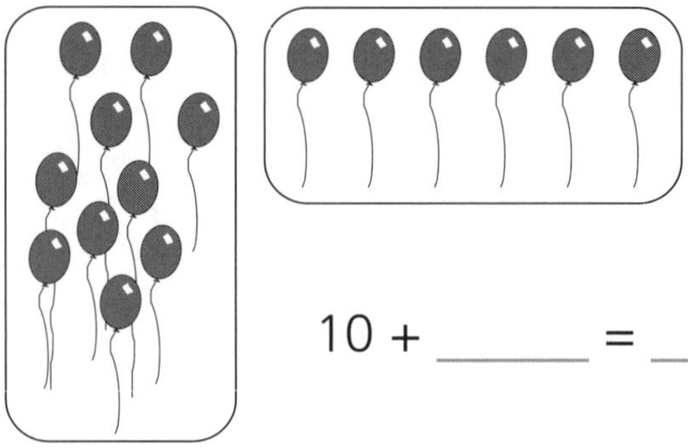

10 + ______ = ______

❽ Write the number shown.

a

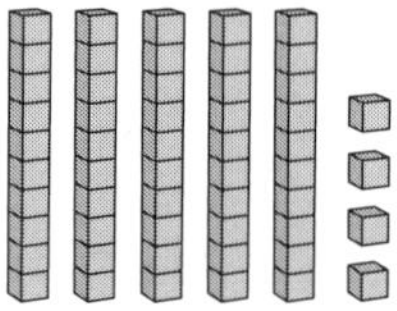

______

☐ tens ☐ ones

b

______

☐ tens ☐ ones

c

5 tens 8 ones

______

❾ Complete the table below.

41		43		
	47		49	

❿ The number before 44: ______

The number after 48: ______

 ISBN 978 0 6557 0882 7

2:2

☐ suns

❶ Use the suns above to answer these questions.

a 2 + 6 = ______ b 4 + 3 = ______ c 4 + 4 = ______

d 3 + 7 = ______ e 8 + 2 = ______ f 3 + 3 = ______

❷ a The __________ is below the scissors.

b The __________ is above the tree.

c The __________ is to the right of the scissors.

d The __________ is between the shoe and tree.

e Circle the objects on the left. Cross the objects on the right.

❸ 5 + 6 ☐ 6 + 6 ☐ 7 + 6 ☐ 7 + 7 ☐ 7 + 8 ☐

2:3

☐ - ☐ = ☐

❶ Complete each number web.

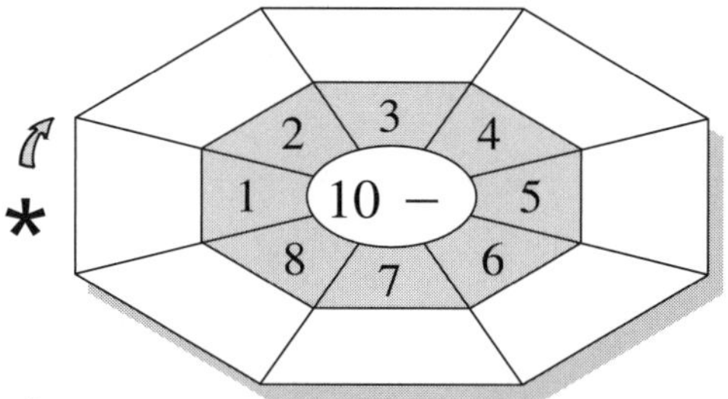

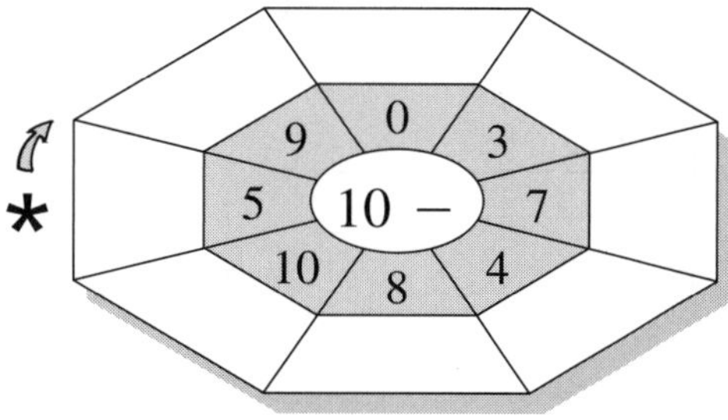

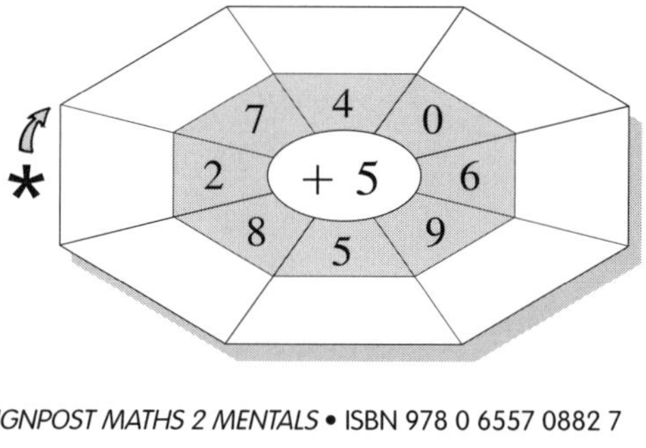

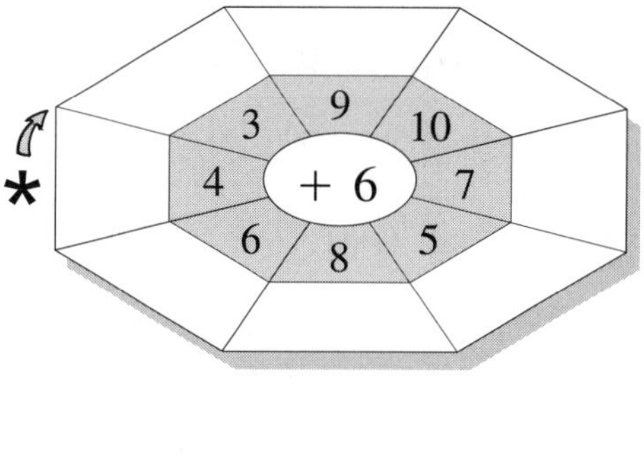

 • • ISBN 978 0 6557 0882 7

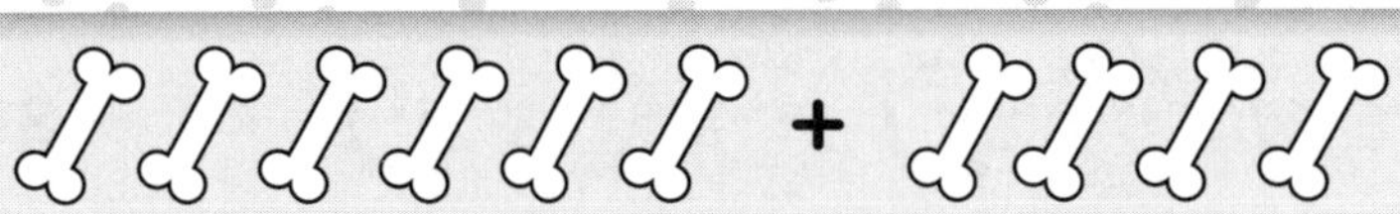

☐ + ☐ = ☐

1

4	1	4	5
+ 1	+ 7	+ 6	+ 5
____	____	____	____

2

6	8	9	7
− 2	− 4	− 8	− 5
____	____	____	____

3 Count on to add 3.

a 14, 15, 16, 17

so 14 + 3 = ____

b 17, 18, ____, ____

so 17 + 3 = ____

4 Write the number after:

a 61 ____ **b** 85 ____

c 47 ____ **d** 93 ____

e 38 ____ **f** 72 ____

5 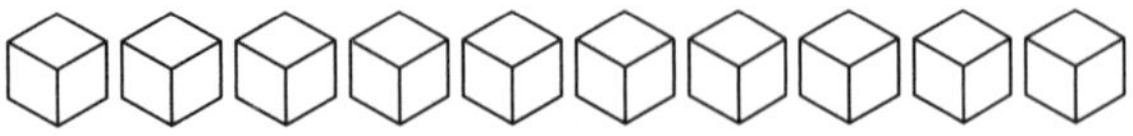

- Colour the 1st block.
- Tick the 4th block.
- Cross out the 9th block.
- Circle the 6th block.

6 Write the number shown.

a 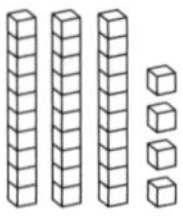 ____

☐ tens ☐ ones

b  ____

☐ tens ☐ ones

7  + 

____ goats + ____ goats

equals ____ goats

8 7 + 7 = ____ 8 + 6 = ____

9 Write 3 different number sentences.

____ + ____ + ____ = 14

____ + ____ + ____ = 14

____ + ____ + ____ = 14

10 

8 − ____ = ____

 AUSTRALIAN SIGNPOST MATHS 2 MENTALS • ISBN 978 0 6557 0882 7

3:2

 ☐ **boats**

❶ Use the boats above to answer these questions.

a 10 – 2 = ______ **b** 10 – 4 = ______ **c** 10 – 7 = ______

d 10 – 5 = ______ **e** 10 – 3 = ______ **f** 10 – 10 = ______

❷ Complete this table.

Coin	Number
5c	
10c	
20c	
50c	

a How many 5c coins? ______

b How many 50c coins? ______

c How many coins altogether? ______

3:3

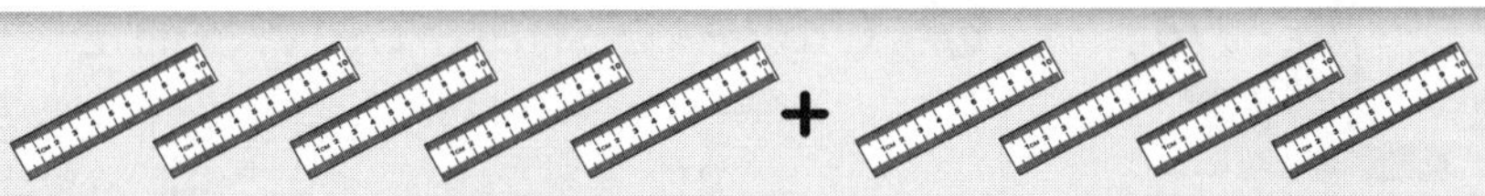 , ☐ + ☐ = ☐

❶ Complete the number bond houses. Each row adds to make the number at the top of the house.

11	
6	
	9
4	
7	
	8
1	

13	
10	
7	
	2
	5
3	
9	

16	
8	
12	
	5
	9
	7
10	

, ☐ + ☐ = ☐

❶ 8 + 4 = ______ 9 + 3 = ______

7 + 5 = ______ 6 + 8 = ______

6 + ______ = 13 8 + ______ = 15

❷

5	7	10	9
+ 6	+ 3	+ 6	+ 4
______	______	______	______

❸ Double 6 = ______

6 + 6 = ______

6 + 5 = ______

6 + 7 = ______

❹

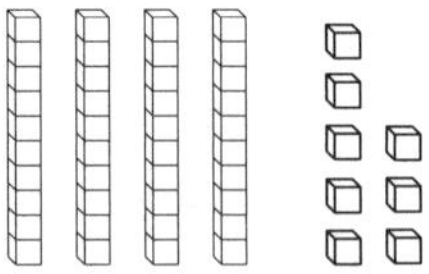

______ tens ______ ones = ______

❺ How many ones blocks make 1 tens block? ______

How many ones blocks make 2 tens blocks? ______

❻ This shape is a ______________.

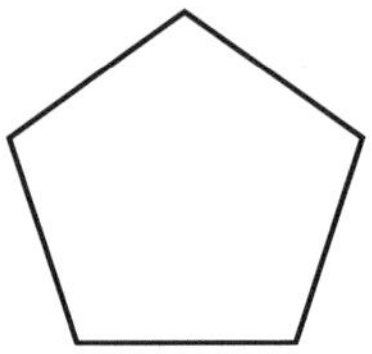

Sides: ______

Vertices: ______

❼ Share 9 counters among the boxes.

☐ ☐ ☐

One share = ______

❽ **a** ______ + ______ = 13

b ______ + ______ + ______ = 8

c ______ + ______ + ______ = 10

❾ Circle to share between 2.

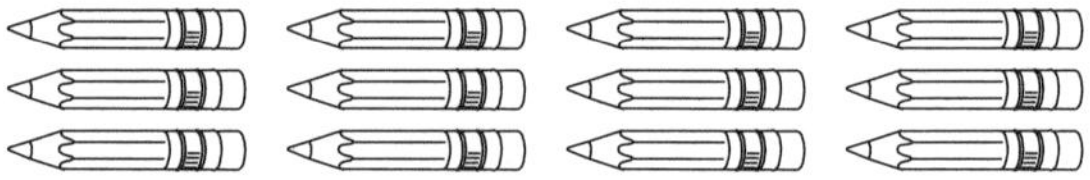

How many pencils? ______

How many shares? ______

How many pencils in each share? ______

❿ Circle the 6th hamburger.
Tick the 1st hamburger.

⓫ This shape is an ______________.

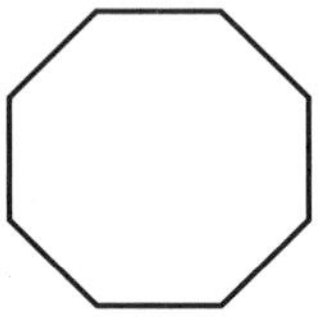

Sides: ______

Vertices: ______

4:2

 +  8 + 3 = ☐

1

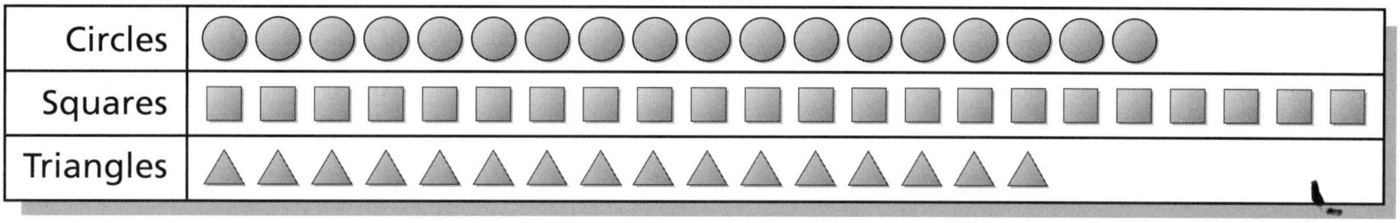

a How many circles and triangles altogether? ______

b How many more squares than circles? ______

c How many more circles than triangles? ______

d How many shapes altogether? ______

4:3

 +  +  = ☐

1 Complete the number bond houses.

How many stars? ☐

15	
13	
	7
	8
11	
	3
2	
5	

17	
11	
10	
	4
	7
9	
5	
	8

18	
9	
3	
	6
	8
	15
11	
7	

19	
	6
2	
13	
	16
11	
	8
9	

5:1

❶ 19 lollies. 8 eaten.
How many are left?

_____ − _____ = _____

❷ Double 5 _____ Double 7 _____

5 + 5 _____ 7 + 7 _____

5 + 6 _____ 7 + 8 _____

5 + 4 _____ 7 + 6 _____

❸ This shape is a ____________.

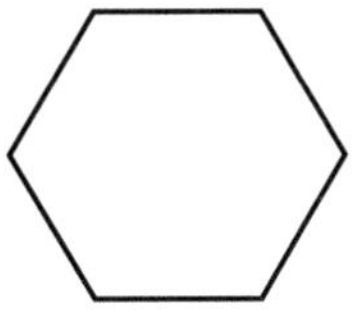

Sides: _____

Vertices: _____

❹ 17 cars. ☐

5 lost. − ☐

How many are left? ☐

❺ Cross out the 9th flower.

❻ 32 = _____ tens _____ ones

❼ Trace the shapes above.
Say out loud the name and how many sides and vertices for each shape.

❽ Share 10 counters among the boxes.

☐ ☐

One share = _____

❾ Circle to share between 3.

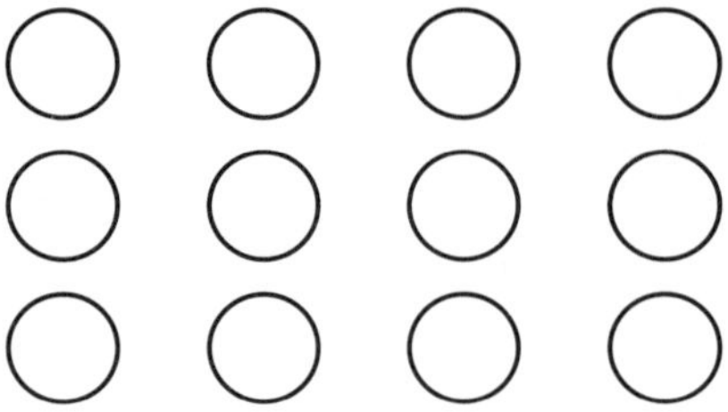

How many counters? _____

How many shares? _____

How many counters in each share? _____

❿ Write the number of vertices for each shape.

_____ _____

5:2 January, February, March, April, May, June, July, August, September, October, November, December

❶

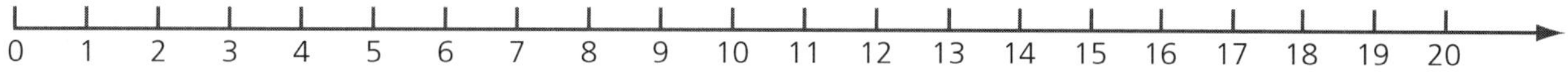

12 – 4 = ______ 17 – 3 = ______ 16 – 5 = ______ 14 – 8 = ______

❷ Complete the missing dates in March.

Colour the 8th, 16th and 24th red.

How many days in March? ______

How many Fridays in March? ______

What day is the 26th of March?

____

March						
Sun	Mon	Tues	Wed	Thurs	Fri	Sat
		1	2	3	4	5
6	7	8	9			
20	21	22	23	24	25	26
27	28	29	30	31		

❸ $5 + 2 =$ ____ $8 + 2 =$ ____ $6 + 3 =$ ____ $4 + 5 =$ ____ $4 + 3 =$ ____

❹ 10 + 2 ☐ 10 + 1 ☐ 10 + 5 ☐ 10 + 3 ☐ 10 + 4 ☐

5:3 56, 57, 58, ____, ____, ____, ____, ____, 64, 65

❶ Fill in the missing numerals.

a 61, 62, ____, ____, ____, ____, 67, ____, ____, ____

b 87, 88, ____, ____, ____, ____, 93, ____, ____, ____

c 48, 49, ____, ____, ____, ____, 54, ____, ____, ____

d 30, 29, ____, ____, ____, ____, 24, ____, ____, ____

Learn the days of the week and the months of the year.

6:1

30 days has September, April, June and November. All the rest have 31 except February alone, which has 28 days clear and 29 days each leap year.

1

12	18	14
− 9	− 3	− 5
____	____	____

2 7 + 5 + 5 = ______

4 + 4 + 3 = ______

6 + 6 + 2 = ______

1 + 3 + 3 = ______

3 + 7 + 7 = ______

3 Circle the 8th crocodile.

4 19 cakes. ☐

5 eaten. − ☐

How many now? ☐

5 Complete these number sentences.

8 + ______ = 15

6 + ______ = 15

11 + ______ = 15

6 How many days in:

a March? ______

b September? ______

c July? ______

7 Look for tens to find:

2	7	9
1	4	1
8	2	5
+ 4	+ 3	+ 5
☐	☐	☐

8 Start at 'Start'. Follow the path and write the letters you pass through. Do not go back to 'Start' for b and c.

	G	S	V	Y	A
	A	P	G	E	D
	T	I	N	K	R
Start		S	A	T	U

a 1 right, 1 up, 1 left ________

b 2 up, 1 right, 1 up ________

c 2 right, 2 up ________

9 Does 3 + 6 = 6 + 3? ______

Does 5 + 7 = 7 + 5? ______

10 65 = ______ tens ______ ones

 ISBN 978 0 6557 0882 7

6:2

 , ☐ – ☐ = ☐

❶

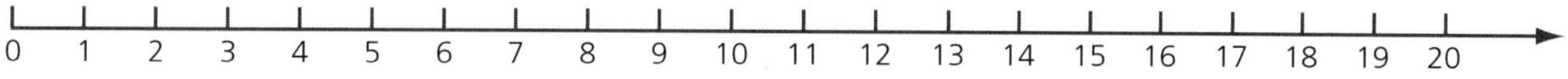

14 – 7 = ______ 15 – 5 = ______ 12 – 3 = ______ 19 – 6 = ______

❷ **a** How many birds? ______

b How many more dogs than cats? ______

c How many animals altogether? ______

Animals in the park

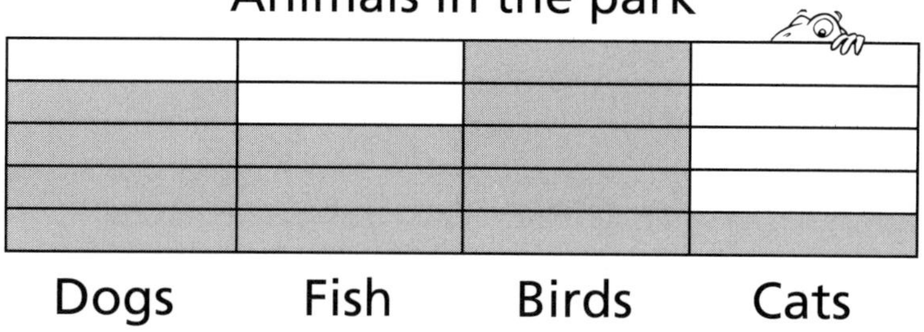

d How many dogs and cats were there at the park? ______

e There are ______ more fish than cats at the park.

❸ Write the number 1 more than: 45 ______ 63 ______ 38 ______

Write the number 1 less than: 36 ______ 57 ______ 72 ______

❹ 6 + 3 ☐ 4 + 3 ☐ 5 + 2 ☐ 7 + 3 ☐ 3 + 3 ☐

6:3

 , ☐ + ☐ = ☐

❶ Complete these addition facts.

	+ 1	+ 2	+ 3	+ 4	+ 5	+ 6	+ 7	+ 8	+ 9
4									

	+ 5	+ 9	+ 2	+ 7	+ 8	+ 1	+ 3	+ 6	+ 4
7									

7:1

❶ Say each clock time above.

❷ 5 + 3 + 3 = ______

8 + 2 + 2 = ______

4 + 4 + 5 = ______

❸ Complete these number sentences.

7 + ______ = 17
9 + ______ = 17
8 + ______ = 17

❹ Look for tens to find:

6	9	2
3	7	4
4	1	8
+ 1	+ 3	+ 3
☐	☐	☐

❺ Draw a line to share 8 stickers between 2 children.

One share = ______

❻ Circle 3 rows of 4.

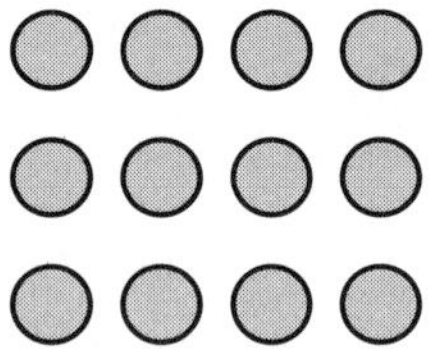

______ + ______ + ______ = ______

______ rows of ______ = ______

❼ Start at 'Start'. Follow the path and write the letters you pass through.

	T	E	T	S	A
	A	R	A	D	S
	R	A	E	P	N
Start		T	R	A	I

a 4 right, 2 up __________

b 3 up, 1 right __________

❽ Circle groups to show how many students could have 2 pears.

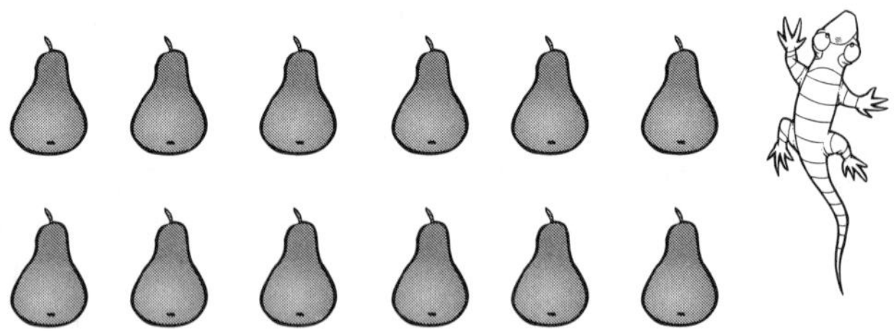

______ students could have 2 pears.

❾ 85 = ______ tens ______ ones

❿ 8 + 1 ☐ 3 + 3 ☐ 3 + 6 ☐ 4 + 3 ☐ 4 + 4 ☐

7:2  , ☐ groups of ☐ = ☐

❶ **a** 

____ rows of ____ = ______

____ + ____ = ______

b  

____ rows of ____ = ______

____ + ____ + ____ = ______

c 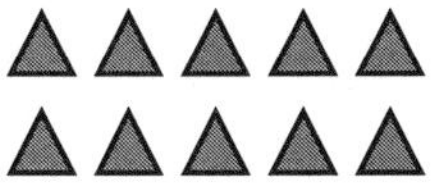

____ rows of ____ = ______

____ + ____ = ______

d 

____ rows of ____ = ______

____ + ____ + ____ = ______

❷ Draw the time shown.

6 o'clock 

half past 3 

quarter past 4 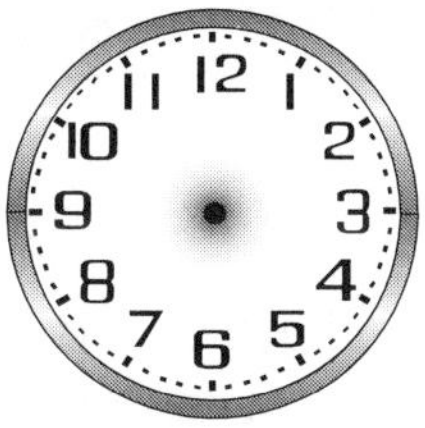

quarter to 11 

❸ At a quarter past, the minute hand has moved ________ minutes around the clock from 12. This is a quarter of the way around the clock.

7:3  +  = ☐ balls

❶ Complete these number sentences for each total.

a
10 + ____ =
8 + ____ =
12 + ____ =
9 + ____ =
16

b
11 + ____ =
7 + ____ =
10 + ____ =
8 + ____ =
13

c
16 + ____ =
9 + ____ =
15 + ____ =
10 + ____ =
20

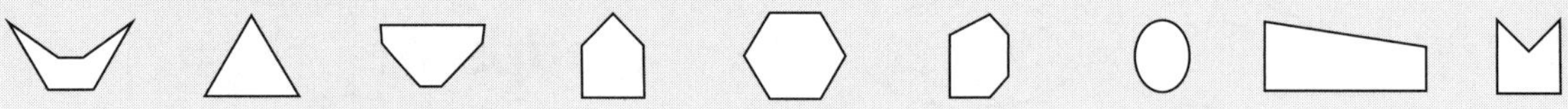

❶ Draw a line to share 10 stars between 2 children.

One share = ______

❷ 12 cars. Circle groups to show how many children could take 4 cars.

______ children could take 4 cars.

❸ Show:

a half past 9 **b** quarter to 3

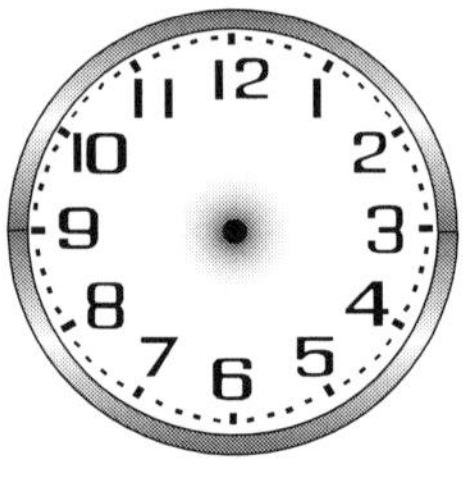

❹

______ groups of ______ = ______

4 + ______ + ______ = ______

❺ Colour all of the hexagons above.

❻ Use a ruler to draw triangles. Start and finish each line at a dot.

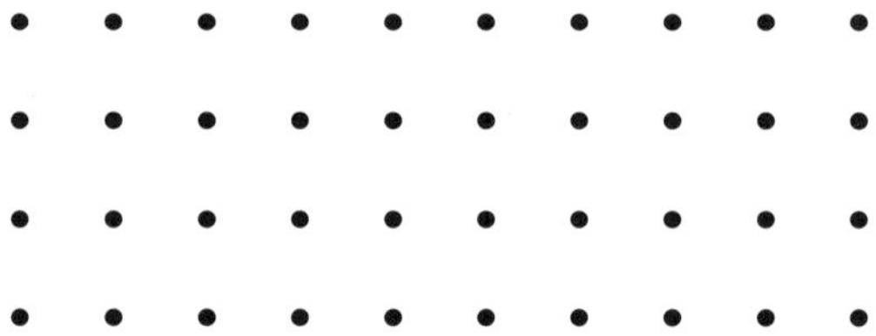

❼ 2 rows of 6 = ______

______ + ______ = ______

❽ Write the time shown.

____

____

____

____

❾ 5 – 2 ______ 10 – 1 ______

8 – 3 ______ 9 – 4 ______

5 – 3 ______ 8 – 2 ______

❿ 6 + 2 ☐ 3 + 4 ☐ 5 + 2 ☐ 5 + 4 ☐ 2 + 1 ☐

 • *AUSTRALIAN SIGNPOST MATHS 2 MENTALS* • ISBN 978 0 6557 0882 7

8:2

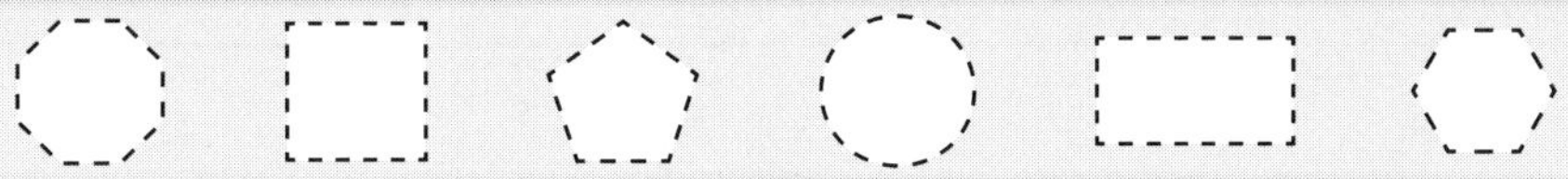

❶ Draw a line to join each shape to its name.

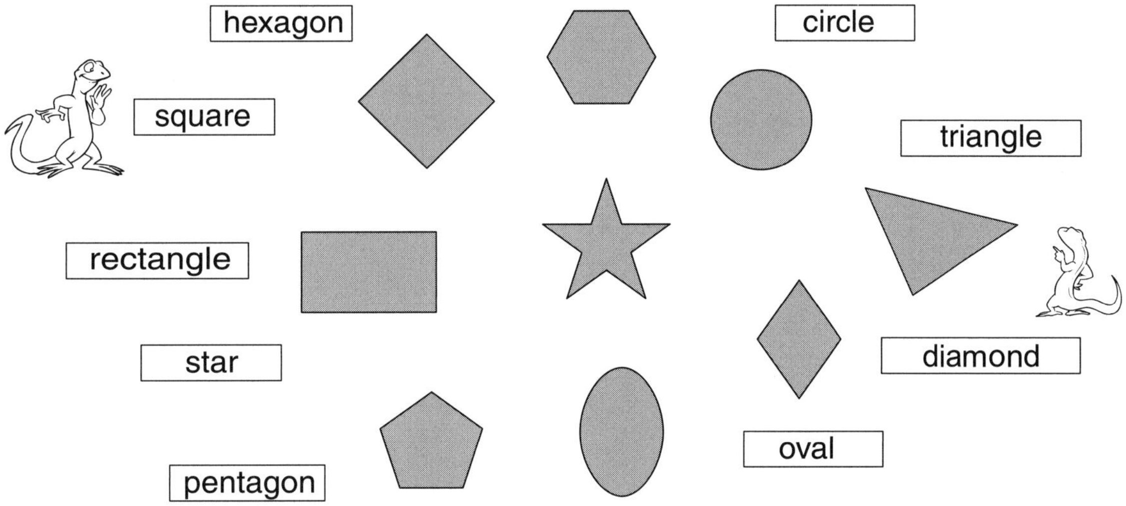

❷ Write the time shown.

a

______

b

______

c

______

d

______

e

______

f

______

Half past nine

Half

Quarter past 11

Quarter

8:3

 , ☐ **groups of** ☐ = ☐

❶

______ groups of ______ = ______

5 + 5 + ______ = ______

❷

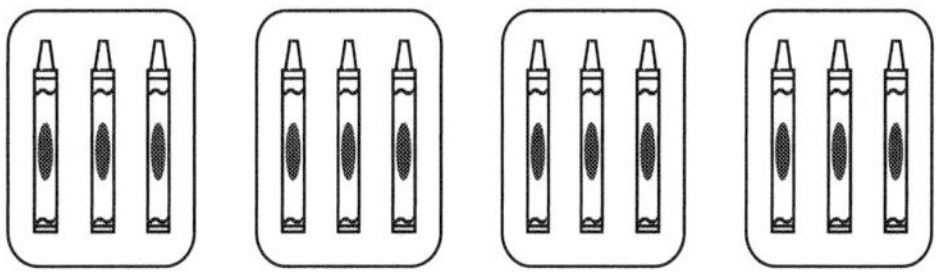

______ groups of ______ = ______

3 + 3 + ______ + ______ = ______

1 Use the number line to find:

10 – 3 = ______ 10 – 7 = ______

8 – 2 = ______ 8 – 5 = ______

6 – 3 = ______ 6 – 4 = ______

10 – 6 = ______ 10 – 8 = ______

2

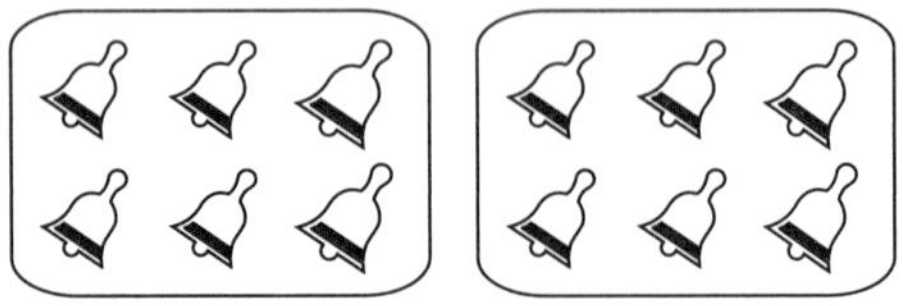

______ groups of ______ = ______

6 + ______ = ______

3

Circle:

The brick is **lighter / heavier** than the book.

4

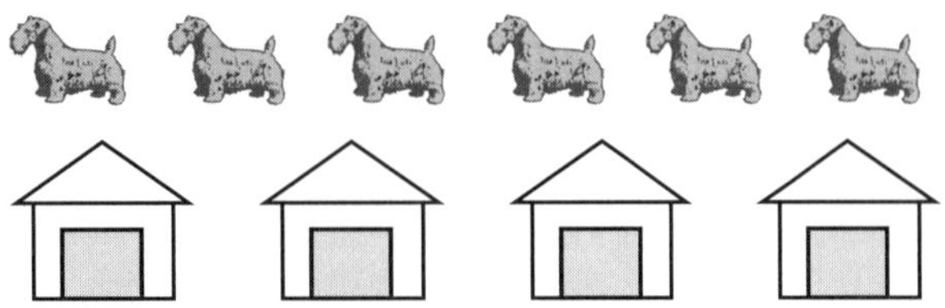

How many more dogs than kennels? ______

5 Use the number line above to find the difference between:

7 and 4 ______ 4 and 3 ______

9 and 7 ______ 6 and 3 ______

6 Use a ruler to draw pentagons. Start and finish each line at a dot.

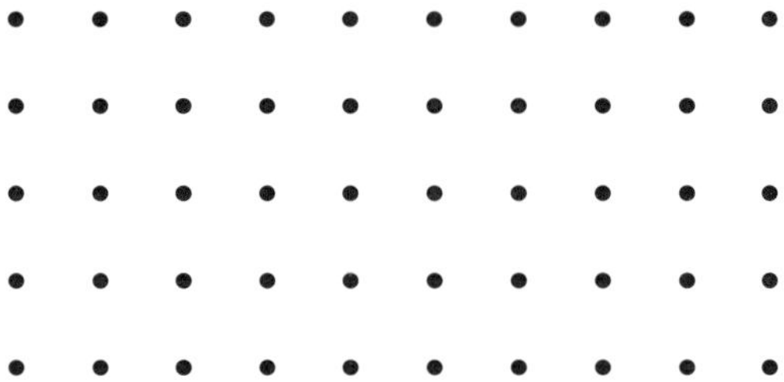

7 Count back to subtract 2.

a 15, 14, ______

so 15 – 2 = ______

b 19, 18, ______

so 19 – 2 = ______

8 A triangle has ____ sides.

An octagon has ____ sides.

9 57 = ______ tens ______ ones

46 = ______ tens ______ ones

9:2

3 groups of 3 = ☐

❶ How many more are needed to make 5?

4 5
3 + 2 = 5

a 0 + ____ = 5

b 1 + ____ = 5

c 4 + ____ = 5

d 2 + ____ = 5

e 5 + ____ = 5

❷ a

_____ rows of _____ = _____

b

_____ groups of _____ = _____

❸ Complete the table to show how many shapes.

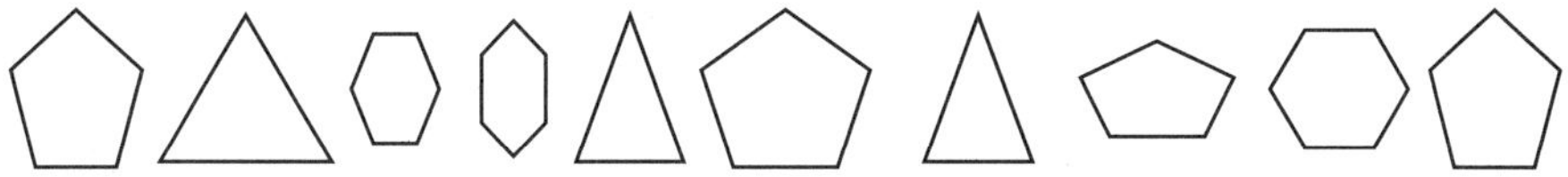

Shape	Number
triangle	
pentagon	
hexagon	

❹ 5 + 3 ☐ 3 + 5 ☐ 2 + 6 ☐ 3 + 2 ☐ 5 + 5 ☐

9:3

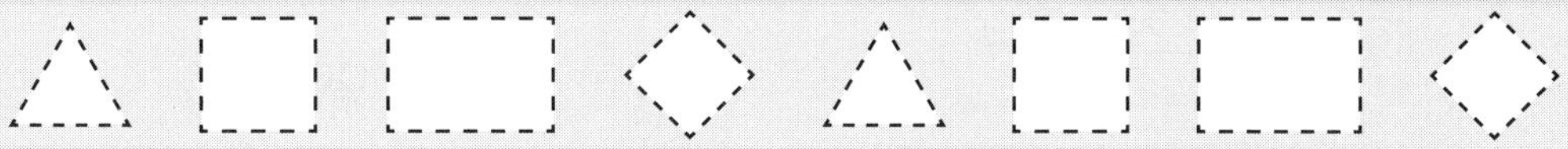

❶ Complete each number web.

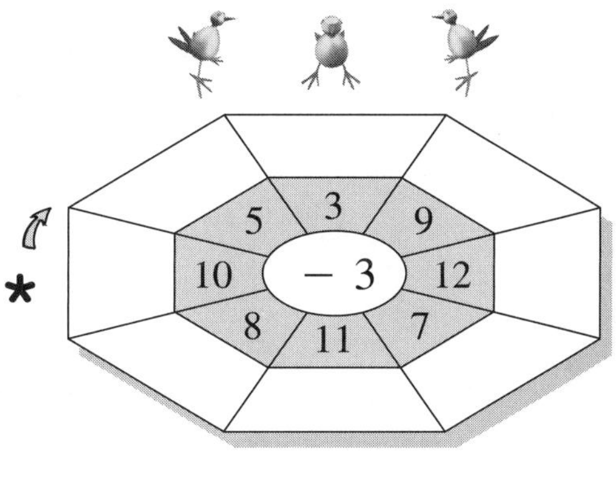

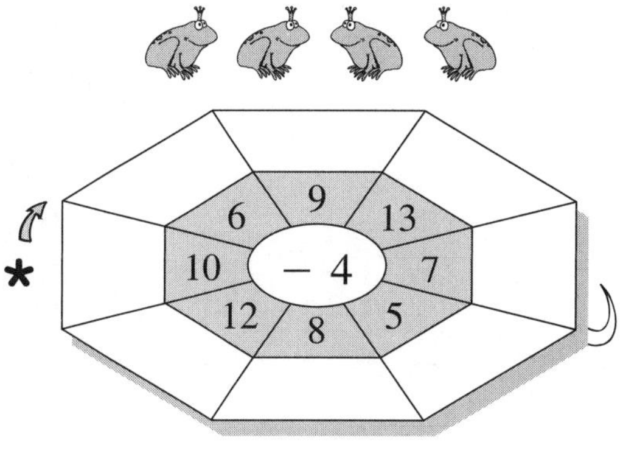

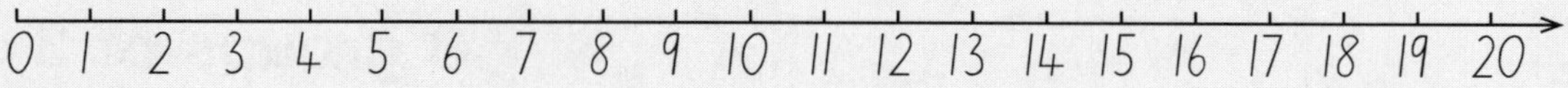

1 Use the number line above to find:

18 – 3 = ______ 18 – 6 = ______

16 – 5 = ______ 16 – 7 = ______

14 – 4 = ______ 14 – 8 = ______

15 – 9 = ______ 17 – 10 = ______

2 Count back to subtract 3.

a 16, 15, ______, ______

so 16 – 3 = ______

b 12, 11, ______, ______

so 12 – 3 = ______

3

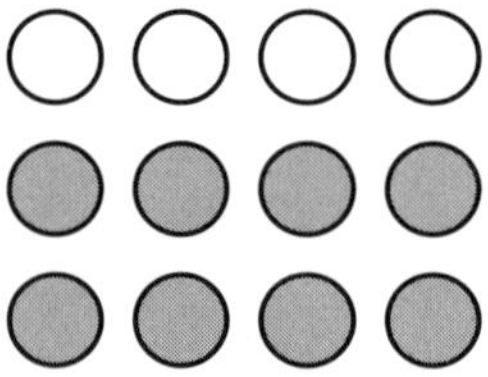

4 + 8 = ______

8 + 4 = ______

12 – 4 = ______

12 – 8 = ______

4 How many squares high is each building?

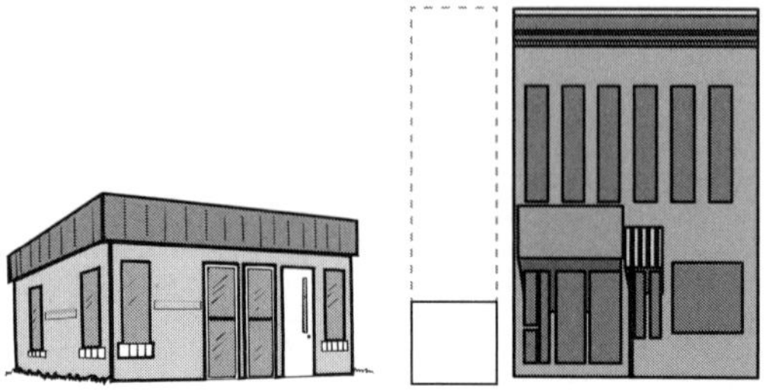

______ squares ______ squares

5 Use the number line above to find the difference between:

a 18 and 15 ______

b 17 and 13 ______

6 Colour the correct arrow.

7

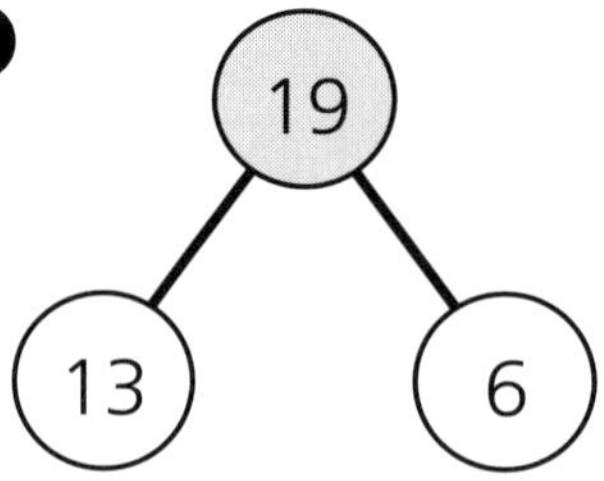

13 + 6 = ______

6 + 13 = ______

19 – 13 = ______

19 – 6 = ______

8

13 altogether. ☐

4 given away. – ☐

How many are left? ☐

9 Write the number 1 more than:

a 24 ______ **b** 56 ______

c 47 ______ **d** 78 ______

10:2

, [ ] – [ ] = [ ]

❶ a

How many dogs? [ ] How many more dogs than rabbits? [ ]

b

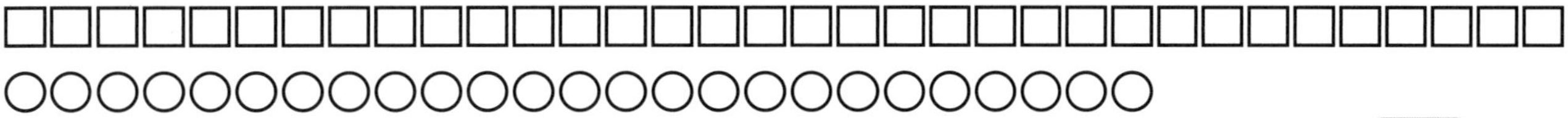

How many squares? [ ] How many more squares than circles? [ ]

❷

18	14	19	17	16
– 9	– 6	– 10	– 8	– 5
____	____	____	____	____

❸ Circle the pencils that have the same length as the one on the left.

❹ 6 + 3 [ ]   7 + 2 [ ]   8 + 3 [ ]   9 + 2 [ ]   6 + 4 [ ]

10:3

, [ ] – [ ] = [ ]

❶ Complete each number web.

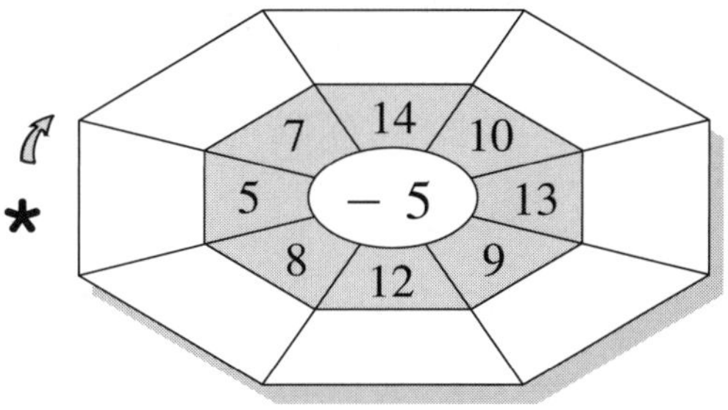

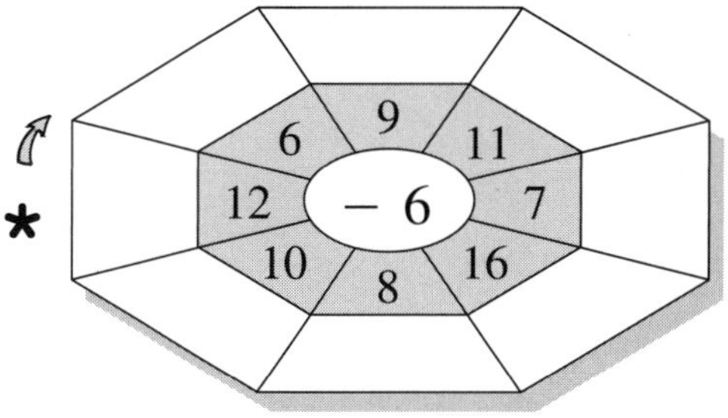

3, 13, 23, ____, ____, ____, ____, ____, ____, ____

❶ 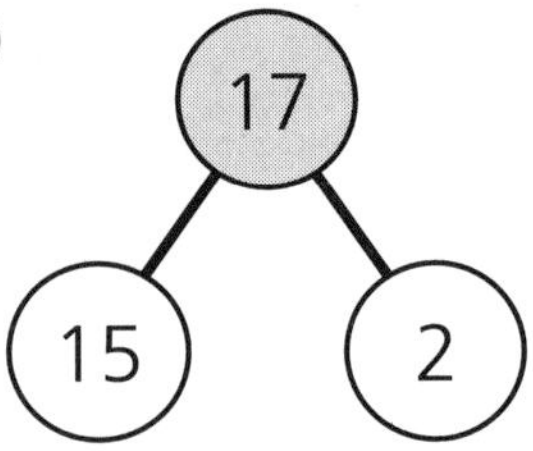

15 + 2 = ____

2 + 15 = ____

17 – 2 = ____

17 – 15 = ____

❷ 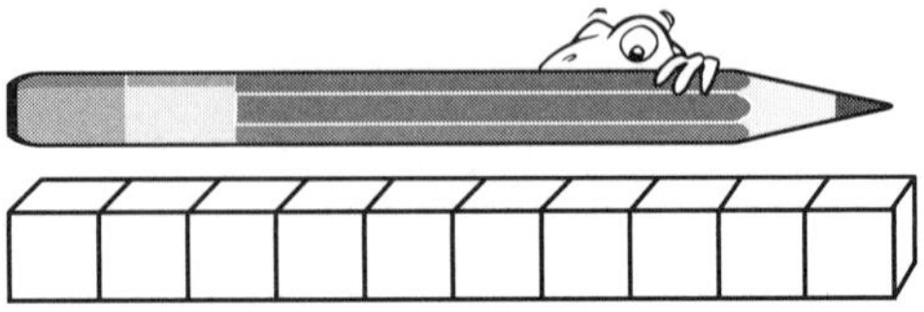

How long is the pencil?

____ blocks

❸ Order the capacity of these containers, **A**, **B** and **C** from smallest to largest.

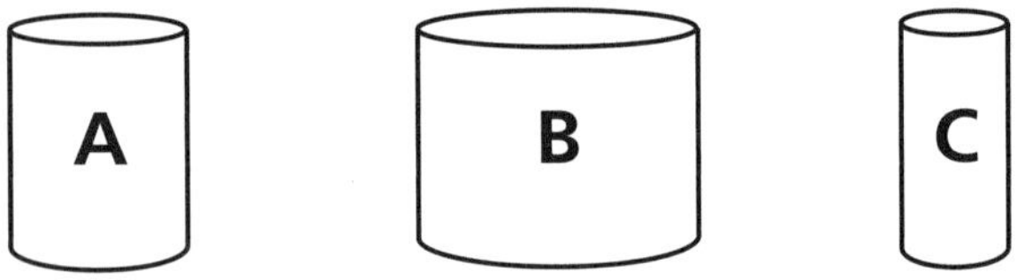

6 cups   12 cups   3 cups

Order: ____________

❹ 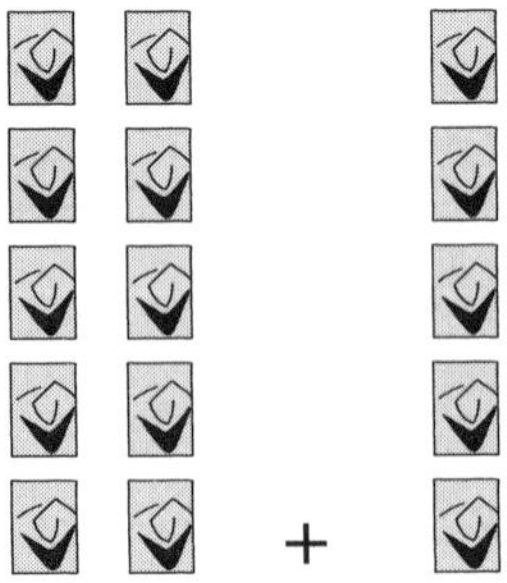

10 + 5 = ____

5 + 10 = ____

15 – 5 = ____

15 – 10 = ____

❺ 15 – 5 = ____   14 – 5 = ____

13 – 3 = ____   13 – 6 = ____

12 – 6 = ____   17 – 8 = ____

❻ The number one less than:

a 46 ____   **b** 72 ____

❼ Add 20 to each number.

a 6 ____   **b** 19 ____

c 23 ____   **d** 47 ____

❽ Add 30 to each number.

a 4 ____   **b** 16 ____

c 37 ____   **d** 65 ____

❾ 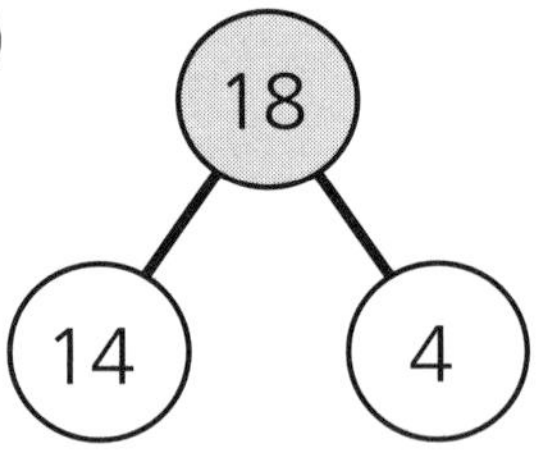

14 + 4 = ____

4 + 14 = ____

18 – 4 = ____

18 – 14 = ____

❿ Write the numeral for forty-three. ____

⓫ 2 + 8 ☐   4 + 4 ☐   5 + 3 ☐   2 + 2 ☐   6 + 4 ☐

11:2

 , ☐ + ☐ = ☐

❶ Colour the boxes that are equal to 7.

17 – 7	12 – 6	10 – 4	18 – 8	11 – 7
10 – 3	11 – 4	15 – 8	13 – 6	12 – 5
11 – 4	9 – 2	16 – 9	11 – 4	10 – 5

❷

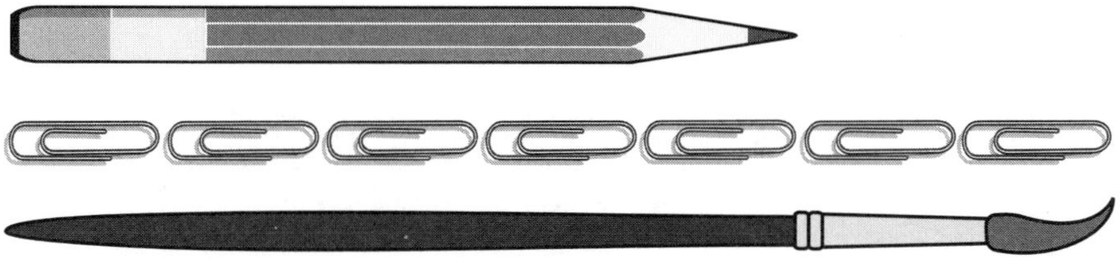

a How long is the pencil? ______ paperclips

b How long is the paintbrush? ______ paperclips

❸ What number is modelled?

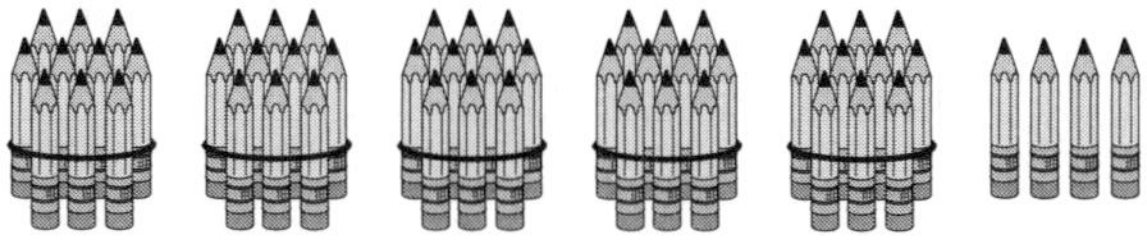

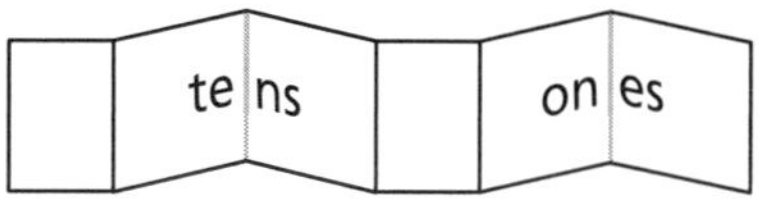

= ______

❹ 1 + 1 ☐ 9 + 0 ☐ 8 + 7 ☐ 5 + 5 ☐ 7 + 4 ☐

11:3

10, 20, 30, 40, 50, 60, ______ , ______ , ______ , ______

❶ Complete each number web.

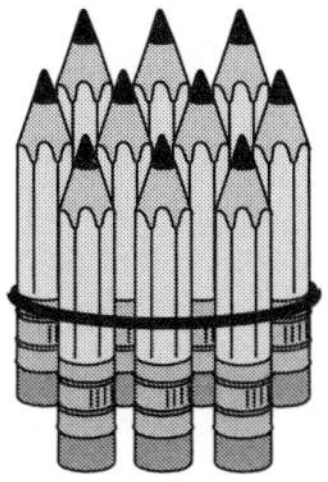

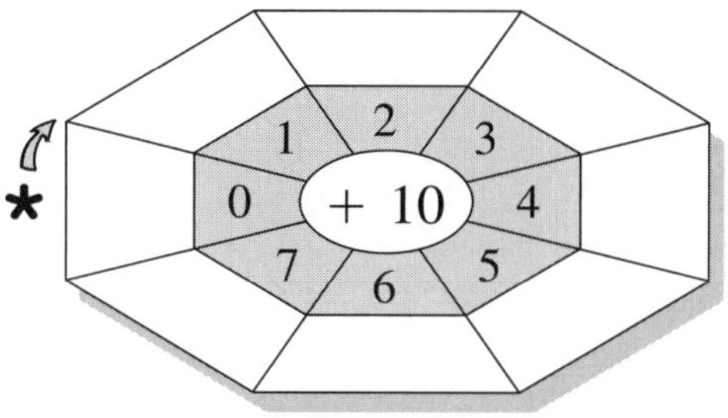

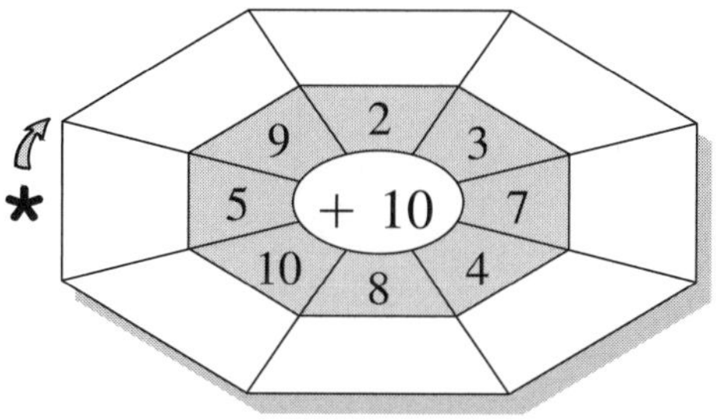

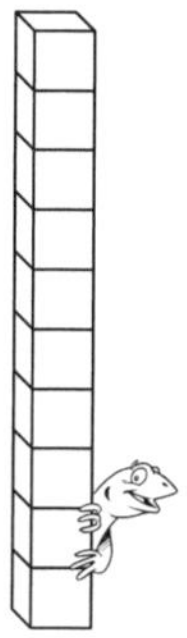

12:1 12, 22, 32, 42, 52, ____, ____, ____, ____

❶ Complete this part of the number chart.

4	5	6	7	
	15			18
24	25			28
34		36	37	
	45		47	48

4 + 10 = ____ 8 + 10 = ____

16 + 10 + 10 = ____

37 – 10 – 10 = ____

❷ 18, 28, 38, ____, ____, ____

15, 25, 35, ____, ____, ____

❸ 

6 + ____ = 10

10 + ____ = 13

10 + ____ = 17

❹ 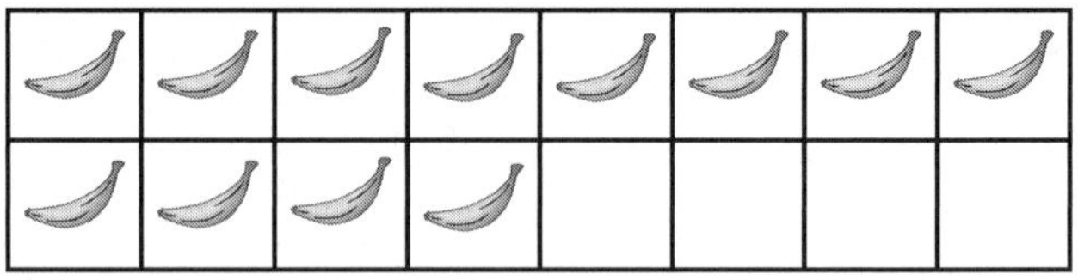

12 + ____ = 16 16 – ____ = 12

❺ Write the number shown.

a  ____ **b**  ____

❻

Container	Number
carton	8 cups
jug	5 cups
pot	10 cups

a Which container holds 10 cups? ____

b How many cups do the jug and pot hold altogether? ____

c Which container holds the least? ____

❼ Add 10 each time to make a pattern.

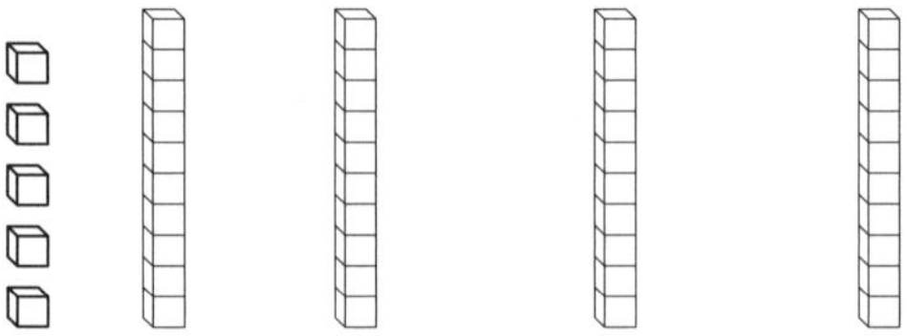

5 , 15, ____, ____, ____

❽ 2 + 5 ☐ 2 + 7 ☐ 3 + 8 ☐ 2 + 4 ☐ 8 + 3 ☐

12:2

□ – □ = □

❶ Find the missing numbers by first counting on to the next ten.

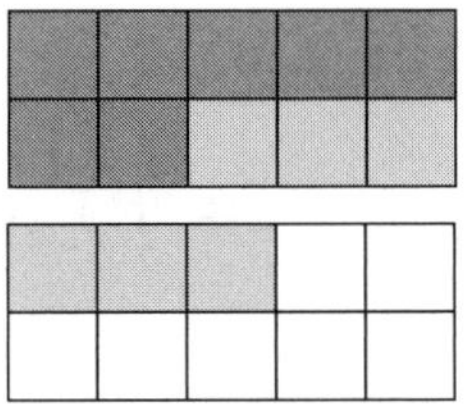

a 4 + ______ = 10 b 16 + ______ = 20

c 8 + ______ = 15 d 19 + ______ = 24

e 18 + ______ = 26 f 17 + ______ = 36

7 + **6** = 7 + (**3** + **3**)
= 13

❷ Colour the boxes that give the answer 8.

11 – 2	4 + 4	13 – 5	7 + 2	12 – 4
1 + 7	10 – 4	4 + 8	16 – 8	2 + 6
10 – 3	7 + 2	14 – 6	5 + 3	16 – 9

❸ Write the missing numbers in each pattern then write the rule.

a 10, 20, ______, 40, ______, ______, 70 Rule ____________

b 4, 14, ______, 34, 44, ______, 64 Rule ____________

c 7, 17, 27, ______, 47, 57, ______ Rule ____________

d 21, ______, 41, 51, ______, 71, 81 Rule ____________

12:3

8, 18, 28, 38, 48, ______, ______, ______, ______

❶ Complete each number web.

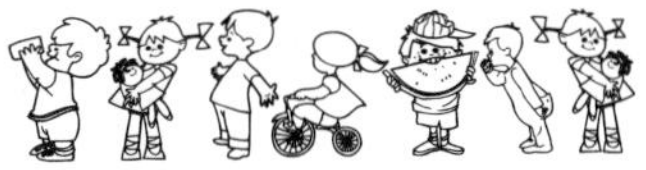

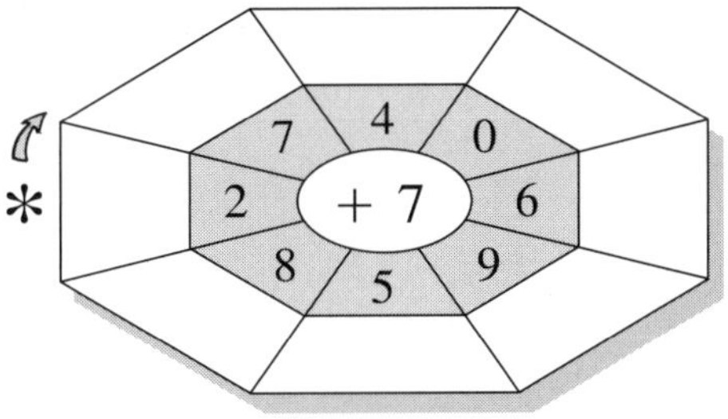

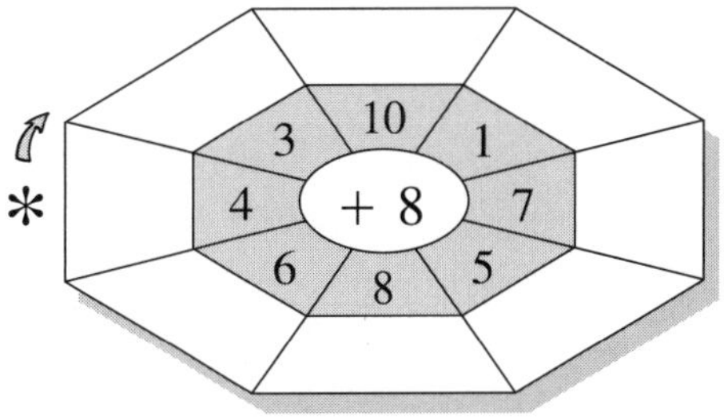

 • *AUSTRALIAN SIGNPOST MATHS 2 MENTALS* • ISBN 978 0 6557 0882 7

 ☐,  ☐,  ☐

❶ 5 + 10 = ______ 7 + 10 = ______

35 + 10 + 10 = ______

87 – 10 = ______

❷ 36, 46, 56, ______, ______, ______

21, 31, 41, ______, ______, ______

❸ Add 10 each time to complete this pattern.

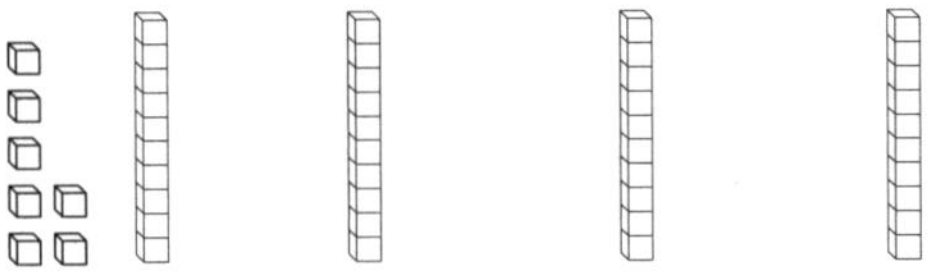

7, 17, ______, ______, ______

❹ Circle the one that takes less time.

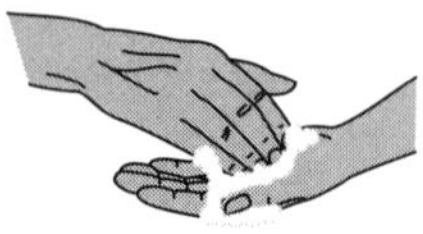

Wash hands

Do the dishes

❺ Draw a line at the halfway point. Colour half of the triangles.

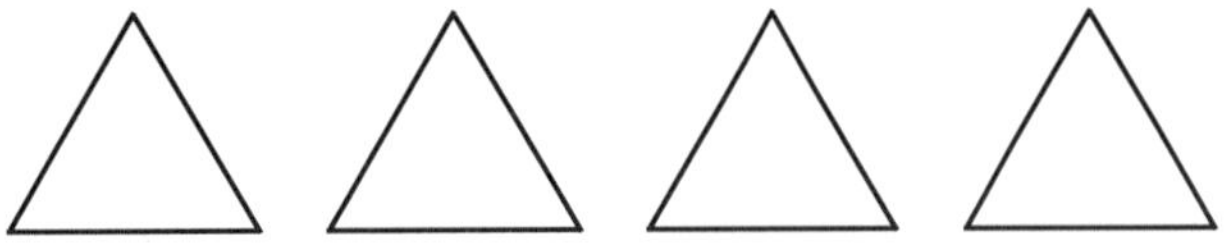

❻ The number one more than:

a 57 ______ **b** 93 ______

❼ How many sides on:

a 2 triangles? ______

b 3 triangles? ______

c 4 triangles? ______

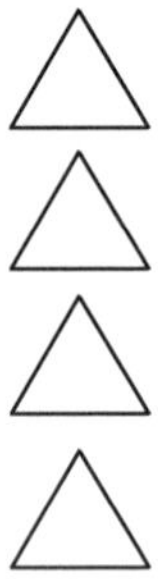

❽ 1 hour = ______ minutes

Half an hour = ______ minutes

❾

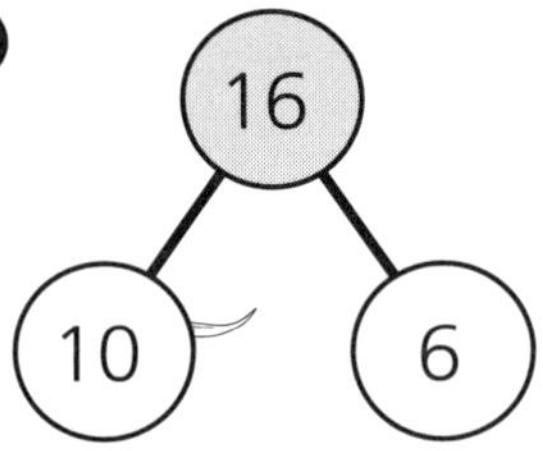

10 + 6 = ______

6 + 10 = ______

16 – 10 = ______

16 – 6 = ______

❿ Write the numeral for sixty-two. ______

⓫ Add 10 to each number.

a 29 ______ **b** 54 ______

c 53 ______ **d** 86 ______

Add 20 to each number.

e 41 ______ **f** 37 ______

g 65 ______ **h** 72 ______

Add 30 to each number.

i 24 ______ **j** 51 ______

⓬ 3 + 3 ☐ 6 + 3 ☐ 6 + 6 ☐ 6 + 9 ☐ 7 + 7 ☐

 • *AUSTRALIAN SIGNPOST MATHS 2 MENTALS* • ISBN 978 0 6557 0882 7

13:2 9, 19, 29, ____, ____, ____, ____, ____, ____, ____

❶ Find the missing numbers by first counting on to the next ten.

a 8 + ____ = 10 **b** 17 + ____ = 20 **c** 28 + ____ = 30

d 6 + ____ = 13 **e** 37 + ____ = 43 **f** 46 + ____ = 54

❷ Use the list to complete the table then the graph. Answer the questions.

Animals in the park

List:
dog, bird, dog
dog, fish, dog,
bird, bird, fish,
cat, bird, bird

Animals in the park

Table:	Tally	Total
Dog		
Fish		
Bird		
Cat		

Graph: **Animals in the park**

Dog	Fish	Bird	Cat

a How many birds? ____

b How many cats? ____

c How many more dogs than cats? ____

d How many animals altogether? ____

❸ Colour half of each group of shapes.

a □ □ □ □ **b** ○ ○ ○ ○ ○ ○ ○ ○ ○ ○ **c** △ ▽ △ ▽ △ ▽

13:3 7, 17, 27, ____, ____, ____, ____, ____, ____, ____

△ △ △ △

❶ Complete each number web.

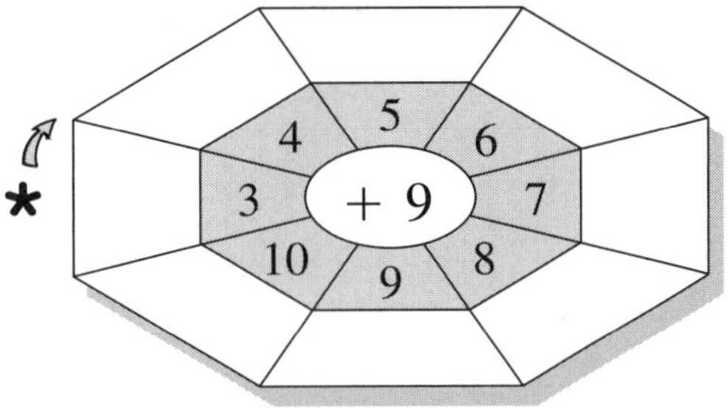

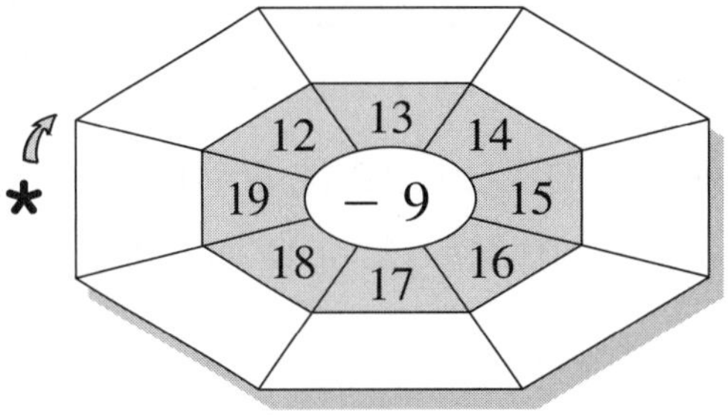

○ ○ ○ ○ ○ ○ Colour half of each group of shapes. □ □

 • *AUSTRALIAN SIGNPOST MATHS 2 MENTALS* • ISBN 978 0 6557 0882 7

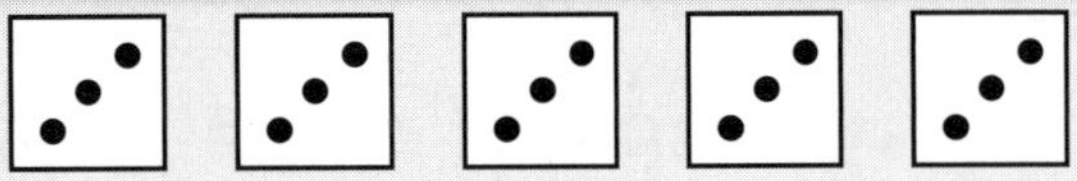

_____ groups of _____ = _____

❶ First count to the next 10 to find:

8 + _____ = 10   15 + _____ = 20

9 + _____ = 17   17 + _____ = 22

27 + _____ = 31   29 + _____ = 34

❷ 

How many legs are there on:

a 2 beetles? _____

b 3 beetles? _____

c 4 beetles? _____

❸ Draw a line at the halfway point of this line of foxes.

Circle one half of the foxes.

❹ Write a number pattern to show the number of sides for each part.

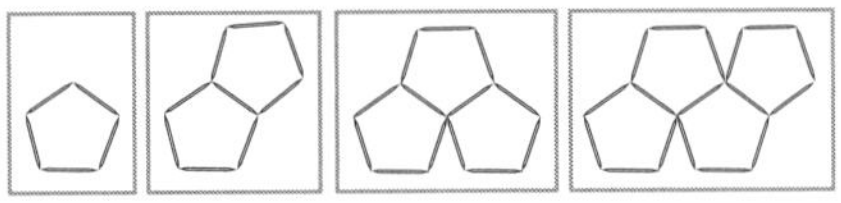

…

5, 9, _____, _____, _____

❺ Would it take a minute or an hour to read a chapter book?

____

❻ The cherries below show

_____ groups of _____ = _____.

_____ × _____ = _____

❼ Colour half of each group.

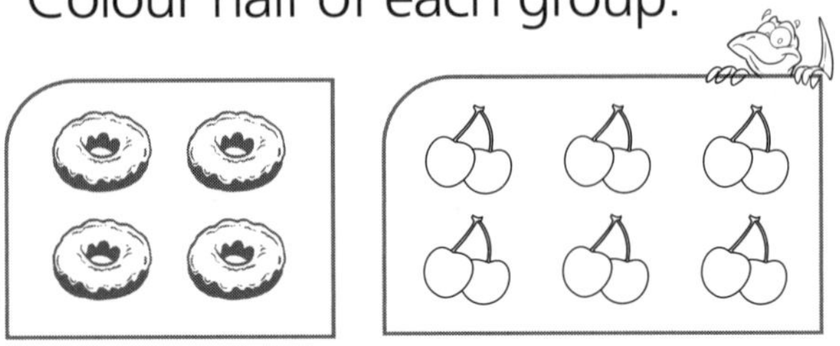

❽ **a** 23, 33, 43, _____, _____, _____

b 32, 42, 52, _____, _____, _____

❾ How many vertices on:

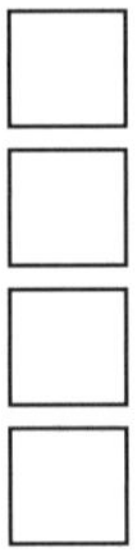

a 2 squares? _____

b 3 squares? _____

c 4 squares? _____

❿ Write the number shown.

a  _____

b  _____

⓫ Double 4.

_____ + _____ = _____

2 × 4 = _____

⓬ 9 + 3 ☐   8 + 5 ☐   7 + 4 ☐   9 + 5 ☐   8 + 4 ☐

 ISBN 978 0 6557 0882 7

14:2  _____ groups of _____ = _____

❶ **a** 1 groups of 5 = ____ **b** 2 group of 5 = ____ **c** 3 groups of 5 = ____

d 1 × 5 = ______ **e** 2 × 5 = ______ **f** 3 × 5 = ______

❷ Use the pictures to finish the graph. Draw a circle to show each animal.

Lives in trees							
Lives on land							
Lives in water							

❸ Continue the number pattern and write the rule to show the number of sides.

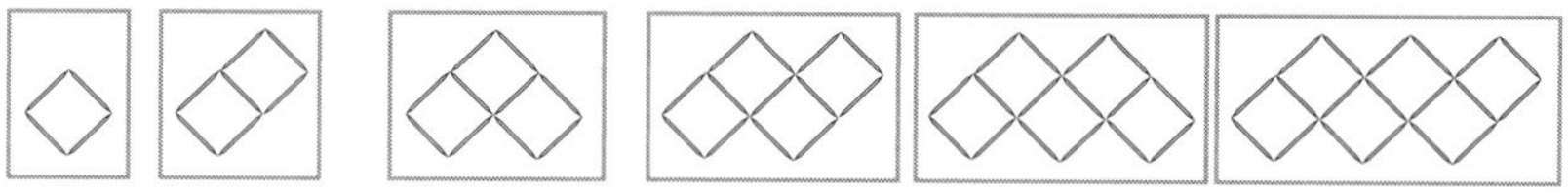

4, ______, ______, ______, ______, ______ Rule: ______

14:3  _____ groups of _____ = _____

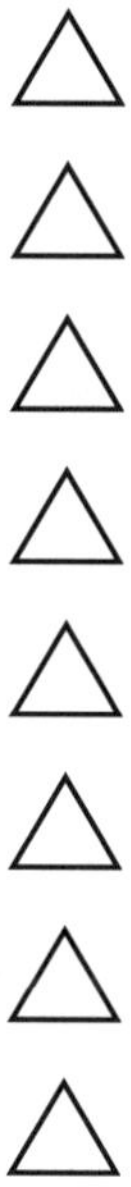

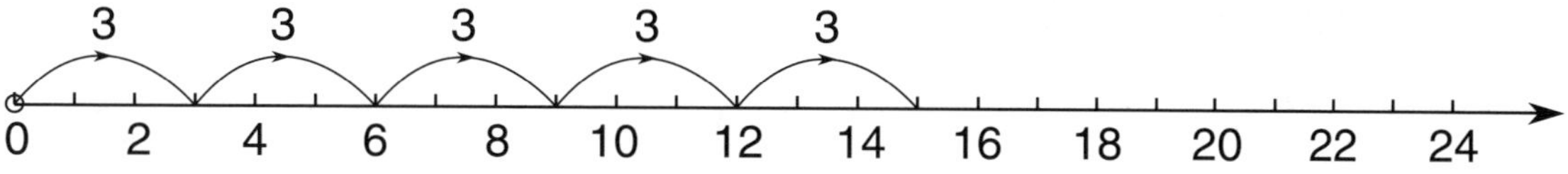

❶ We can use a number line to find **groups of** or **rows of**.
5 groups of 3 = 15

a 3 groups of 3 = ______ **b** 4 rows of 3 = ______

c 4 groups of 2 = ______ **d** 5 rows of 2 = ______

e 7 × 3 = ______ **f** 5 × 3 = ______

g 6 × 3 = ______ **h** 3 × 2 = ______

'×' means groups of.

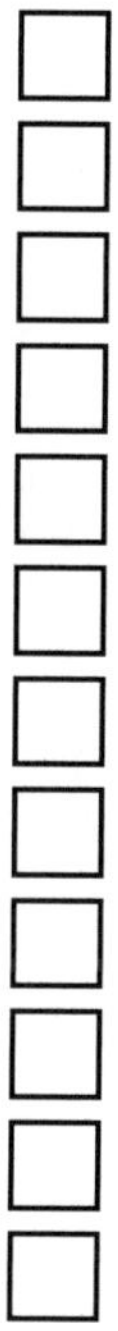

 Colour half of each group.

_____ groups of _____ = _____

❶ Write the number modelled.

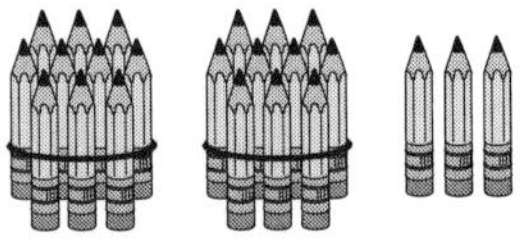

_____

❷ Draw three groups of two flowers.

_____ groups of _____ = _____

_____ × _____ = _____

❸ True or false:

3 × 2 = 2 × 3? _____________

❹ Start with the highest value and count on to find how much money?

____

❺ **a** Match each coin to its name.

50c	$2	20c	$1

b Colour the gold coins yellow.

❻

4 × 2 horns = _____ horns

____ + ____ + ____ + ____ = ____

❼ How much money?

_____ cents

❽ Use this array to answer:

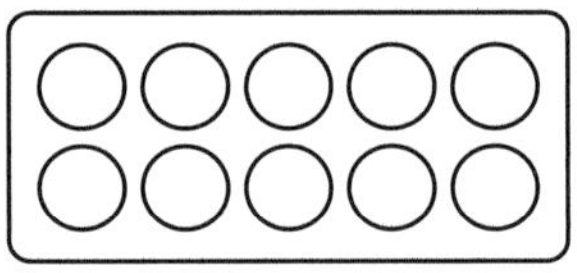

2 × 5 = _____

_____ rows of _____ = _____

Number of fives in 10 = _____

❾ Draw 5 rows of 2 balls.

5 × 2 = _____

Do 2 rows of 5 and 5 rows of 2 have the same total?

____

 • *AUSTRALIAN SIGNPOST MATHS 2 MENTALS* • ISBN 978 0 6557 0882 7

15:2

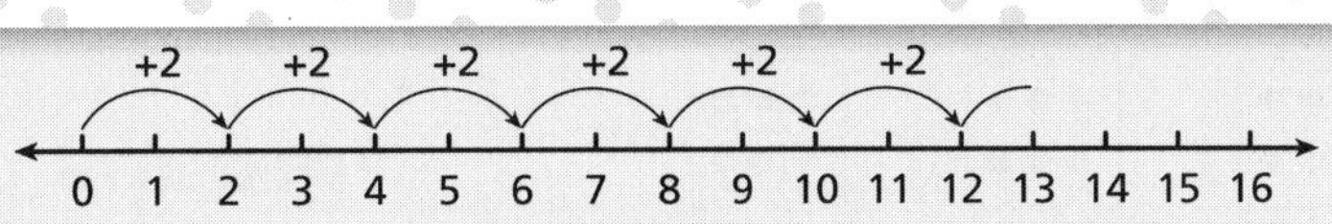

1 **a** 3 groups of 2 = ______

2 + 2 + 2 = ______

3 × 2 = ______

b 5 groups of 2 = ______

2 + 2 + 2 + 2 + 2 = ______

5 × 2 = ______

c 2, 4, 6, ______, ______, ______, ______, ______, ______

2 Use this grid to draw arrays and answer the questions.

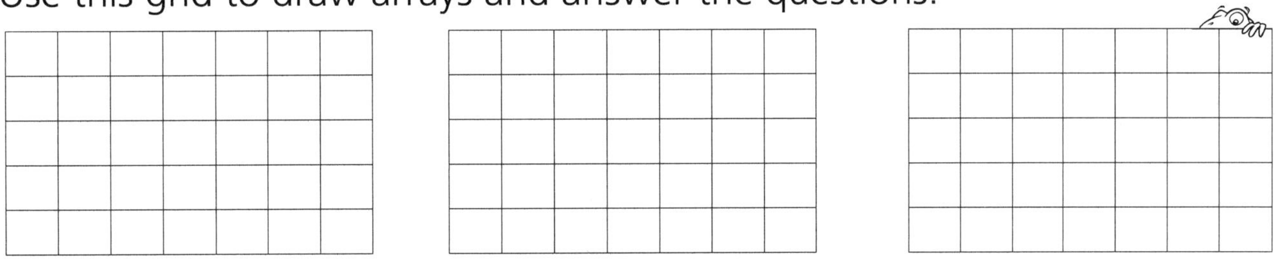

a 2 rows of 4 ______

4 columns of 2 ______

2 × 4 = ______

4 × 2 = ______

b 3 rows of 5 ______

5 columns of 3 ______

3 × 5 = ______

5 × 3 = ______

c 4 rows of 6 ______

6 columns of 4 ______

4 × 6 = ______

6 × 4 = ______

15:3

18, 16, 14, ______, ______, ______, ______, ______, ______

1 Continue each pattern.

a 2, 4, 6, 8, ______, ______, ______, ______

b 22, 24, 26, ______, ______, ______, ______

c 5, 10, 15, ______, ______, ______, ______

d 10, 20, 30, ______, ______, ______, ______

e 100, 110, 120, ______, ______, ______

[ ] groups of ten dots = [ ]

_____ groups of _____ = _____

1. Double 8 = ____ + ____ = ____

   2 × 8 = ____

2. How much money? ________

3. 2, 4, 6, _____, _____, _____, _____

4. 

   _____ groups of _____ = _____

   _____ × _____ = _____

5. What number is shown? ______

   Which number is next? ______

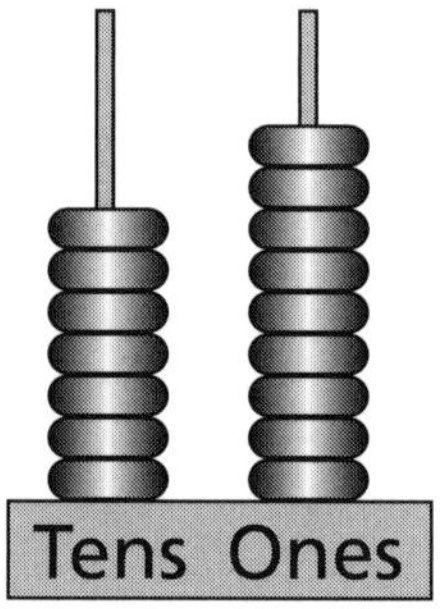

6. How many in 3 rows of 5? ______

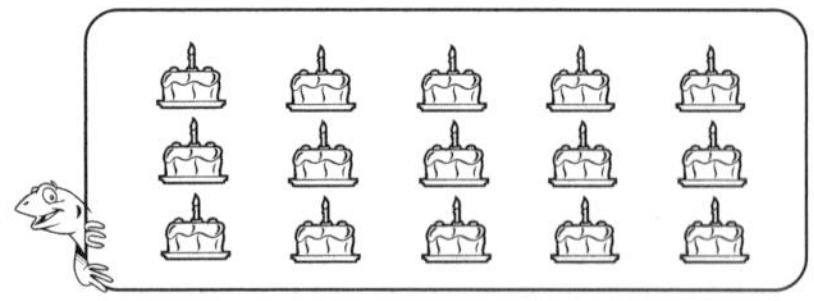

3 rows of 5 = 5 columns of 3

True or false? ______

7. 3, 6, 9, _____, _____, _____, _____

8. Describe this array.

2 × 3 = _____

_____ rows of _____ = _____

Number of threes in 6 = _____

9. 3 rows of 2 = _____

True or false?

2 × 3 = 3 × 2 ____________

10. Show a quarter past 5 on the clock.

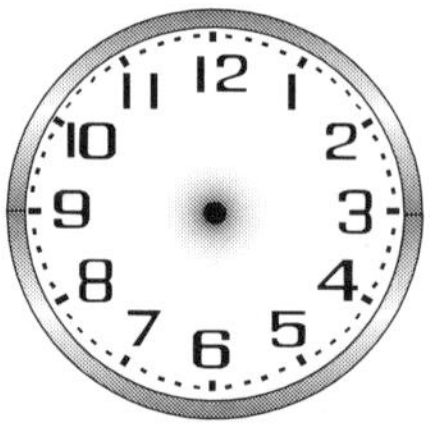

11. This time is:

____

____

12. 

_____ groups of _____ cats

= _____ cats altogether

3 × 8 = _____

 • *AUSTRALIAN SIGNPOST MATHS 2 MENTALS* • ISBN 978 0 6557 0882 7

16:2

, ☐ – ☐ = ☐

❶ **a** 5, 10, 15, ____, ____, ____, ____, ____, ____, ____, ____, ____

b 3, 6, 9, ____, ____, ____, ____, ____, ____, ____, ____, ____

❷ Use this grid to draw arrays and find each total.

a 3 rows of 5 = ____

$3 \times 5 =$ ____

$5 \times 3 =$ ____

b 4 rows of 3 = ____

$3 \times 4 =$ ____

$4 \times 3 =$ ____

c 2 rows of 6 = ____

$2 \times 6 =$ ____

$6 \times 2 =$ ____

❸ Draw 3 groups of 5 balls.

☐ ☐ ☐

3 groups of 5 = ____

$3 \times 5 =$ ____

16:3

, ☐ **groups of** ☐ = ☐

10, 20, ☐, 40, ☐, 60, ☐, 80, ☐

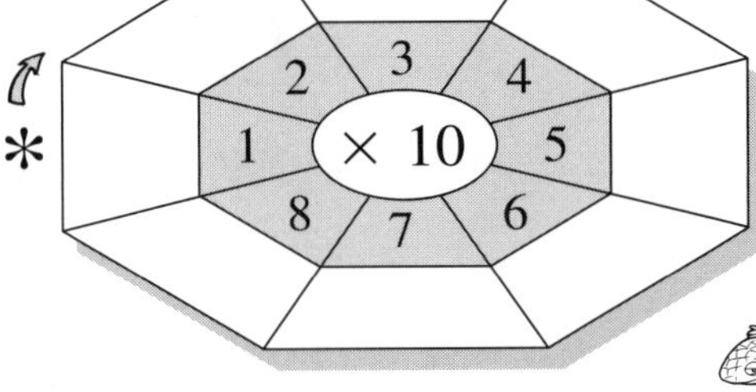

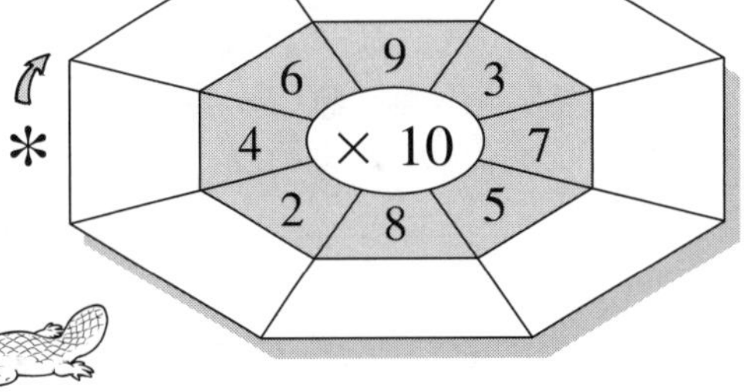

 • *AUSTRALIAN SIGNPOST MATHS 2 MENTALS* • ISBN 978 0 6557 0882 7

❶ Look at the faces above.

a How many faces? ______

b How many groups? ______

c How many faces in each group? ______

d ______ groups of _____ = ______

e Is 3 groups of 4 faces the same number as 4 groups of 3 faces?

____

❷ Double 3

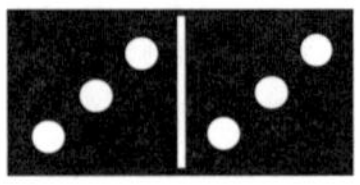

______ + ______ = ______

2 × ______ = ______

❸ How much money? __________

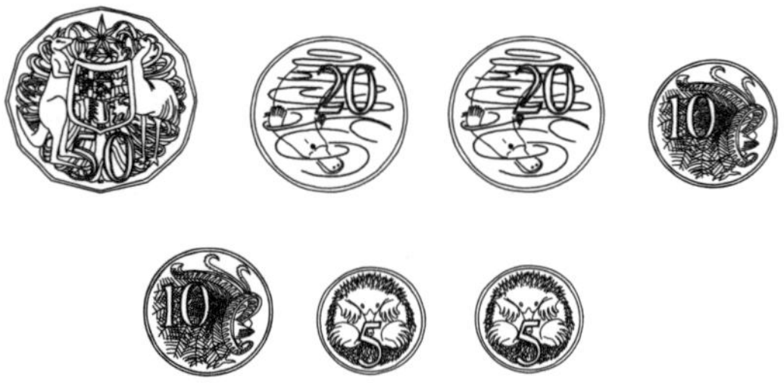

❹ How many are in 2 rows of 7?

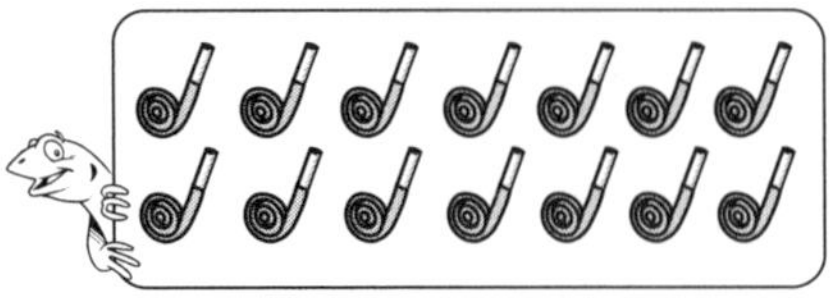

____

2 rows of 7 = 7 rows of 2

True or false? ______________

❺ 2, 4, 6, _____, _____, _____, _____

❻

______ groups of _____ = ______

______ × _____ = ______

❼ Write the number modelled.

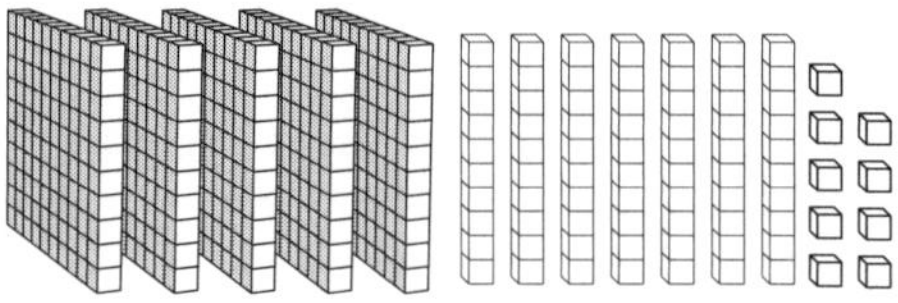

______

❽ a 7 hundreds + 5 tens + 3 ones

= ______

b 6 hundreds + 2 tens + 5 ones

= ______

c 2 hundreds + 9 tens + 2 ones

= ______

❾

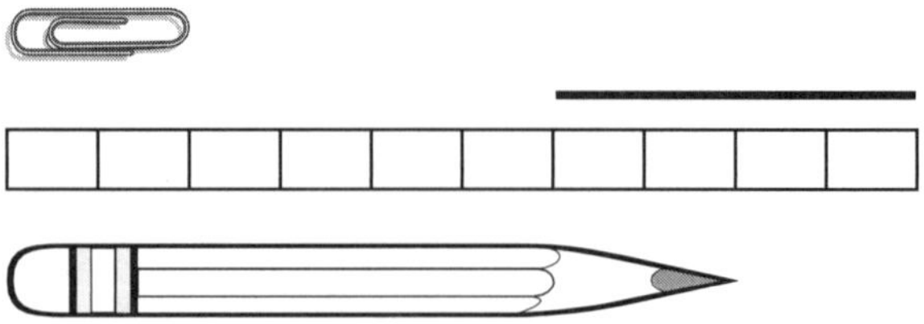

How many paperclips are the same length as:

a the pencil? ______

b the black line? ______

 AUSTRALIAN SIGNPOST MATHS 2 MENTALS • ISBN 978 0 6557 0882 7

Answers

ID card A

1 place-value blocks **2** numeral expander **3** abacus **4** number line **5** number bond **6** add (addition) or plus **7** take away, subtract or minus **8** multiplication sign **9** division sign **10** is equal to **11** number sentence **12** ordinal numbers **13** even numbers **14** odd numbers **15** money **16** dollars **17** cents **18** one half **19** one quarter **20** one eighth **21** groups of **22** rows of **23** reflection or flip **24** slide **25** turn **26** left hand **27** right hand **28** picture graph **29** table **30** tally

ID card B

1 circle **2** oval **3** triangle **4** square **5** rectangle **6** pentagon **7** hexagon **8** octagon **9** quadrilaterals **10** parallel lines, angle **11** area is 6 squares **12** line of symmetry **13** sphere **14** cube **15** cylinder **16** cone **17** prism **18** face **19** vertex **20** edge **21** curved surface **22** flat surface **23** analog clock **24** digital clock **25** 4 o'clock **26** half past 8 **27** quarter past 3 **28** quarter to 4 **29** calendar **30** balance scales

1:1

6

1 **a** 5 **b** 12

2 7, 6, 7, 5 **3** 6

4 **a** 15 **b** 10 **c** 12 **d** 3 **e** 19

5 2, 2 **6** 2 + 3 = 5

7 **a** 6 circles will be drawn in each box. One share = 6 circles.

b 8 squares will be drawn in each box. One share = 8 squares.

8 5 + 5 = 10 **9** 7 (days)

10 3, 6, 13, 2

11 4, 5, 6, 5, 7

1:2

9 − 4 = 5

1 **a**

b 12

2 A square, a pentagon, a hexagon and an octagon will be drawn on the grid to match each label. For example:

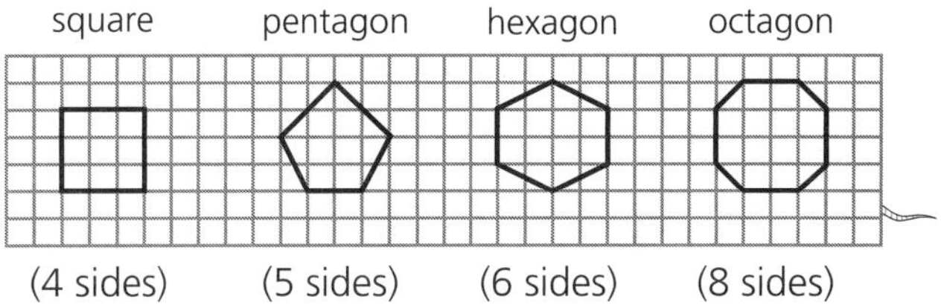

3 6, 9, 7, 8, 10

1:3

7 + 4 = 11

1 27, 50 **2** 31, 20

3

1	2	3	4	5	6	7	8	9	10
11	12	13	14	15	16	17	18	19	20
21	22	23	24	25	26	27	28	29	30
31	32	33	34	35	36	37	38	39	40
41	42	43	44	45	46	47	48	49	50

2:1

10 + 2 = 12

1 5, 9, 4, 9 **2** 6, 5, 3, 5 **3** 10, 8, 12 **4** left

5 12 + 6 = 18 **6** 7, 4, 10 **7** 10 + 6 = 16

8 **a** 54, 5 tens 4 ones

b 32, 3 tens 2 ones **c** 58

9

41	42	43	44	45
46	47	48	49	50

10 43, 49

2:2

10 (suns)

❶ **a** 8 **b** 7 **c** 8 **d** 10 **e** 10 **f** 6

❷ **a** ball **b** pen **c** pen **d** ball **e** The yo-yo and the shoe will be circled. The pen and the tree will be crossed.

❸ 11, 12, 13, 14, 15

2:3

9 – 3 = 6

❶ 9, 8, 7, 6, 5, 4, 3, 2
5, 1, 10, 7, 3, 6, 2, 0
7, 12, 9, 5, 11, 14, 10, 13
10, 9, 15, 16, 13, 11, 14, 12

3:1

6 + 4 = 10

❶ 5, 8, 10, 10 ❷ 4, 4, 1, 2

❸ **a** 14, 15, 16, 17, 14 + 3 = 17

b 17, 18, 19, 20, 17 + 3 = 20

❹ **a** 62 **b** 86 **c** 48 **d** 94 **e** 39 **f** 73

❺ 

❻ **a** 34, 3 tens 4 ones

b 51, 5 tens 1 ones

❼ 3 goats + 4 goats equals 7 goats ❽ 14, 14

❾ Answers will vary. One answer could be 10 + 3 + 1 = 14.

❿ 8 – 3 = 5

3:2

10 (boats)

❶ **a** 8 **b** 6 **c** 3 **d** 5 **e** 7 **f** 0

❷

Coin	Number
5c	2
10c	3
20c	1
50c	2

a 2 **b** 2 **c** 8

3:3

5 + 4 = 9

❶

11	
6	5
2	9
4	7
7	4
3	8
1	10

13	
10	3
7	6
11	2
8	5
3	10
9	4

16	
8	8
12	4
11	5
7	9
9	7
10	6

4:1

5 + 4 = 9

❶ 12, 12, 12, 14, 7, 7

❷ 11, 10, 16, 13

❸ 12, 12, 11, 13

❹ 4 tens 8 ones = 48

❺ 10, 20

❻ pentagon, 5 (sides), 5 (vertices)

❼ 3 counters will be drawn in each box.
One share = 3

❽ Answers will vary.
One answer for **a** could be 6 + 7 = 13.
One answer for **b** could be 3 + 4 + 1 = 8.
One answer for **c** could be 4 + 4 + 2 = 10.

❾ Two groups of 6 pencils will be circled. 12 (pencils), 2 (shares), 6 (pencils in each share)

❿ 

⓫ octagon, 8 (sides), 8 (vertices)

4:2

8 + 3 = 11

❶ **a** 34 **b** 4 **c** 2 **d** 56

 • *AUSTRALIAN SIGNPOST MATHS 2 MENTALS* • ISBN 978 0 6557 0882 7

4:3

18

1

15	
13	2
8	7
7	8
11	4
12	3
2	13
5	10

17	
11	6
10	7
13	4
10	7
9	8
5	12
9	8

18	
9	9
3	15
12	6
10	8
3	15
11	7
7	11

19	
13	6
2	17
13	6
3	16
11	8
11	8
9	10

14 (stars)

5:1

1 19 – 8 = 11   2 10, 14, 10, 14, 11, 15, 9, 13

3 hexagon, 6 (sides), 6 (vertices)

4 17
– 5
12 (cars)

5    6 3 tens 2 ones

7 The shapes in the header will be traced.
Circle (1 side, 0 vertices), square (4 sides, 4 vertices), rectangle (4 sides, 4 vertices), pentagon (5 sides, 5 vertices), hexagon (6 sides, 6 vertices), octagon (8 sides, 8 vertices)

8 5 counters will be drawn in each box.
One share = 5

9 Groups of 4 counters will be circled. 12, 3, 4

10 3, 4

5:2

1 8, 14, 11, 6

2

March						
Sun	Mon	Tues	Wed	Thurs	Fri	Sat
		1	2	3	4	5
6	7	8	9	10	11	12
13	14	15	16	17	18	19
20	21	22	23	24	25	26
27	28	29	30	31		

The grey squares will be coloured red, 31 (days), 4 (Fridays), Saturday

3 7, 10, 9, 9, 7   4 12, 11, 15, 13, 14

5:3

56, 57, 58, 59, 60, 61, 62, 63, 64, 65

1 **a** 61, 62, 63, 64, 65, 66, 67, 68, 69, 70
b 87, 88, 89, 90, 91, 92, 93, 94, 95, 96
c 48, 49, 50, 51, 52, 53, 54, 55, 56, 57
d 30, 29, 28, 27, 26, 25, 24, 23, 22, 21

6:1

1 3, 15, 9   2 17, 11, 14, 7, 17

3 

4 19
– 5
14 (cakes)

5 8 + 7 = 15,   6 + 9 = 15,   11 + 4 = 15

6 **a** 31 **b** 30 **c** 31

7

2	7	9
1	4	1
8	2	5
+ 4	+ 3	+ 5
15	16	20

8 **a** SIT **b** TAPS **c** SANG

9 **a** yes **b** yes   10 6 tens 5 ones

6:2

7 – 3 = 4

1 7, 10, 9, 13

2 **a** 5 **b** 3 **c** 13 **d** 5 **e** 2

3 46, 64, 39, 35, 56, 71   4 9, 7, 7, 10, 6

6:3

10 + 2 = 12

1

	+ 1	+ 2	+ 3	+ 4	+ 5	+ 6	+ 7	+ 8	+ 9
4	5	6	7	8	9	10	11	12	13

	+ 5	+ 9	+ 2	+ 7	+ 8	+ 1	+ 3	+ 6	+ 4
7	12	16	9	14	15	8	10	13	11

 • *AUSTRALIAN SIGNPOST MATHS 2 MENTALS* • ISBN 978 0 6557 0882 7

7:1

1. 6 o'clock, 2 o'clock, 9 o'clock, 10 o'clock, 12 o'clock, 4 o'clock, 7 o'clock, 1 o'clock, 8 o'clock, 11 o'clock, 3 o'clock, 5 o'clock
2. 11, 12, 13
3. 7 + 10 = 17, 9 + 8 = 17, 8 + 9 = 17
4.

6	9	2
3	7	4
4	1	8
+ 1	+ 3	+ 3
14	20	17

5. 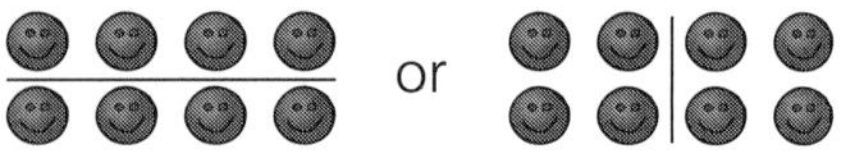 One share = 4
6. 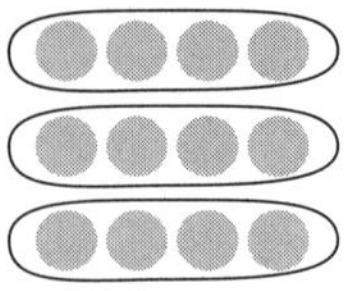 4 + 4 + 4 = 12

   3 rows of 4 = 12
7. **a** TRAINS **b** RATE
8. 6 groups of 2 pears will be circled. 6
9. 8 tens 5 ones
10. 9, 6, 9, 7, 8

7:2

2 groups of 3 = 6

1. **a** 2 rows of 7 = 14, 7 + 7 = 14 **b** 3 rows of 6 = 18, 6 + 6 + 6 = 18

   c 2 rows of 5 = 10, 5 + 5 = 10 **d** 3 rows of 5 = 15, 5 + 5 + 5 = 15
2. 
3. 15

7:3

16 (balls)

1. **a** 10 + 6 = 16, 8 + 8 = 16, 12 + 4 = 16, 9 + 7 = 16

   b 11 + 2 = 13, 7 + 6 = 13, 10 + 3 = 13, 8 + 5 = 13

   c 16 + 4 = 20, 9 + 11 = 20, 15 + 5 = 20, 10 + 10 = 20

8:1

1. 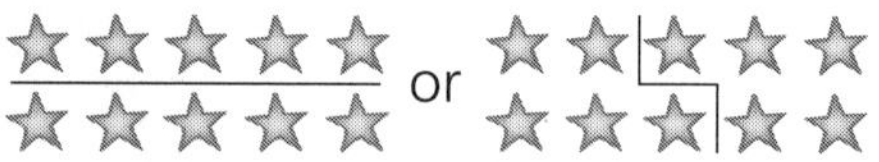 One share = 5
2. 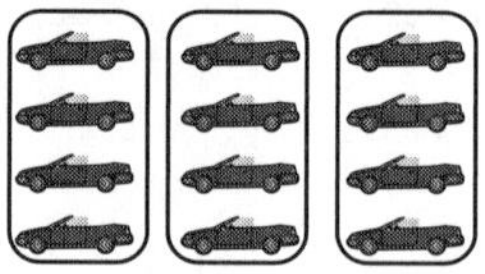 3 (children)
3. **a**  **b** 
4. 3 groups of 4 = 12, 4 + 4 + 4 = 12
5. The 4 hexagons in the header will be coloured.

   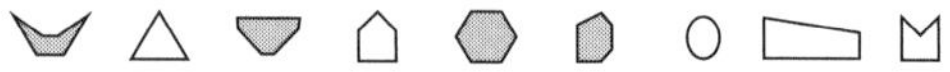
6. Triangles will be drawn.
7. 12, 6 + 6 = 12
8. 2 o'clock (or 2:00)

   5 fifteen, quarter past 5 (or 5:15)
9. 3, 9, 5, 5, 2, 6
10. 8, 7, 7, 9, 3

8:2

The shapes in the header will be traced.

1. 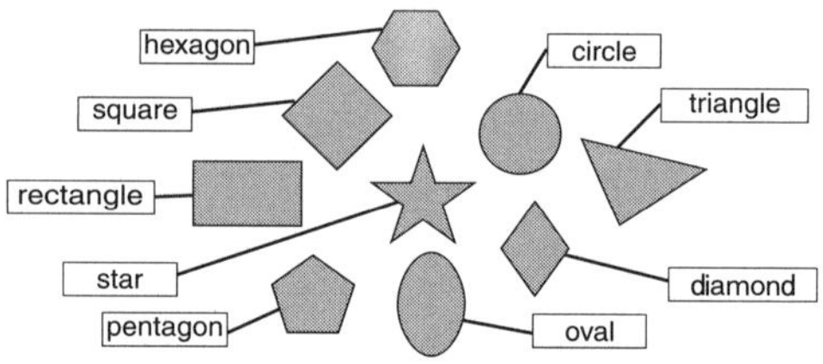

2. **a** half past 8 or 8 thirty

   b half past 12 or 12 thirty

   c half past 5 or 5 thirty

   d quarter to 12 or 11 forty-five

   e quarter past 6 or 6 fifteen

   f quarter to 3 or 2 forty-five

8:3

3 groups of 3 = 9

1. 3 groups of 5 = 15, 5 + 5 + 5 = 15
2. 4 groups of 3 = 12, 3 + 3 + 3 + 3 = 12

9:1

1. 7, 3, 6, 3, 3, 2, 4, 2
2. 2 groups of 6 = 12, 6 + 6 = 12
3. heavier 4. 2 5. 3, 1, 2, 3
6. Pentagons will be drawn.
7. **a** 15, 14, 13 so 15 – 2 = 13
   b 19, 18, 17 so 19 – 2 = 17
8. 3, 8 9. 5 tens 7 ones, 4 tens 6 ones

9:2

3 groups of 3 = 9

1. **a** 0 + 5 = 5 **b** 1 + 4 = 5 **c** 4 + 1 = 5
   d 2 + 3 = 5 **e** 5 + 0 = 5
2. **a** 3 rows of 6 = 18 **b** 4 groups of 10 = 40
3.

Shape	Number
triangle	3
pentagon	4
hexagon	3

4. 8, 8, 8, 5, 10

9:3

The shapes in the header will be traced.

1. 7, 2, 0, 6, 9, 4, 8, 5
   6, 2, 5, 9, 3, 1, 4, 8

10:1

1. 15, 12, 11, 9, 10, 6, 6, 7
2. **a** 16, 15, 14, 13 so 16 – 3 = 13
   b 12, 11, 10, 9 so 12 – 3 = 9
3. 12, 12, 8, 4
4. 2 (squares), 5 (squares)
5. **a** 3 **b** 4
6. 
7. 19, 19, 6, 13
8. 13
   – 4
   9 (stars)
9. **a** 25 **b** 57 **c** 48 **d** 79

10:2

8 – 2 = 6

1. **a** 19, 4 **b** 34, 9 2. 9, 8, 9, 9, 11
3. 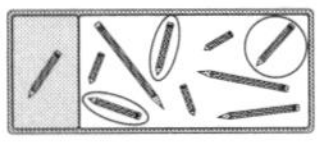
4. 9, 9, 11, 11, 10

10:3

8 – 5 = 3

1. 0, 2, 9, 5, 8, 4, 7, 3
   6, 0, 3, 5, 1, 10, 2, 4

11:1

3, 13, 23, 33, 43, 53, 63, 73, 83, 93

1. 17, 17, 15, 2 2. 10 (blocks)
3. C, A, B 4. 15, 15, 10, 5
5. 10, 9, 10, 7, 6, 9 6. **a** 45 **b** 71
7. **a** 26 **b** 39 **c** 43 **d** 67
8. **a** 34 **b** 46 **c** 67 **d** 95
9. 18, 18, 14, 4 10. 43 11. 10, 8, 8, 4, 10

11:2

7 + 3 = 10

1.

17 – 7	12 – 6	10 – 4	18 – 8	11 – 7
10 – 3	11 – 4	15 – 8	13 – 6	12 – 5
11 – 4	9 – 2	16 – 9	11 – 4	10 – 5

2. **a** 5 (paperclips) **b** 7 (paperclips)
3. 5 tens 4 ones = 54 4. 2, 9, 15, 10, 11

11:3

10, 20, 30, 40, 50, 60, 70, 80, 90, 100

1. 10, 11, 12, 13, 14, 15, 16, 17
   15, 19, 12, 13, 17, 14, 18, 20

 • *AUSTRALIAN SIGNPOST MATHS 2 MENTALS* • ISBN 978 0 6557 0882 7

12:1

12, 22, 32, 42, 52, 62, 72, 82, 92

❶

4	5	6	7	8
14	15	16	17	18
24	25	26	27	28
34	35	36	37	38
44	45	46	47	48

14, 18, 36, 17

❷ 18, 28, 38, 48, 58, 68

15, 25, 35, 45, 55, 65

❸ 6 + 4 = 10, 10 + 3 = 13, 10 + 7 = 17

❹ 12 + 4 = 16, 16 – 4 = 12

❺ **a** 5 **b** 8

❻ **a** the pot **b** 15 (cups) **c** the jug

❼ 5, 15, 25, 35, 45

❽ 7, 9, 11, 6, 11

12:2

9 – 3 = 6

❶ **a** 6 **b** 4 **c** 7 **d** 5 **e** 8 **f** 19

❷

11 – 2	4 + 4	13 – 5	7 + 2	12 – 4
1 + 7	10 – 4	4 + 8	16 – 8	2 + 6
10 – 3	7 + 2	14 – 6	5 + 3	16 – 9

❸ **a** 10, 20, 30, 40, 50, 60, 70; Rule: add 10

b 4, 14, 24, 34, 44, 54, 64; Rule: add 10

c 7, 17, 27, 37, 47, 57, 67; Rule: add 10

d 21, 31, 41, 51, 61, 71, 81; Rule: add 10

12:3

8, 18, 28, 38, 48, 58, 68, 78, 88

❶ 9, 14, 11, 7, 13, 16, 12, 15

12, 11, 18, 9, 15, 13, 16, 14

13:1

5, 9, 7

❶ 15, 17, 55, 77

❷ 36, 46, 56, 66, 76, 86 21, 31, 41, 51, 61, 71

❸ 7, 17, 27, 37, 47

❹ Washing hands will be circled.

❺ ▲ ▲ | △ △

❻ **a** 58 **b** 94 ❼ **a** 6 **b** 9 **c** 12

❽ 60 (minutes), 30 (minutes)

❾ 16, 16, 6, 10 ❿ 62

⓫ **a** 39 **b** 64 **c** 63 **d** 96 **e** 61 **f** 57

g 85 **h** 92 **i** 54 **j** 81

⓬ 6, 9, 12, 15, 14

13:2

9, 19, 29, 39, 49, 59, 69, 79, 89, 99

❶ **a** 2 **b** 3 **c** 2 **d** 7 **e** 6 **f** 8

❷ Table: **Animals in the park**

	Tally	Total
Dog	||||	4
Fish	||	2
Bird	𝍸	5
Cat	|	1

Graph: **Animals in the park**

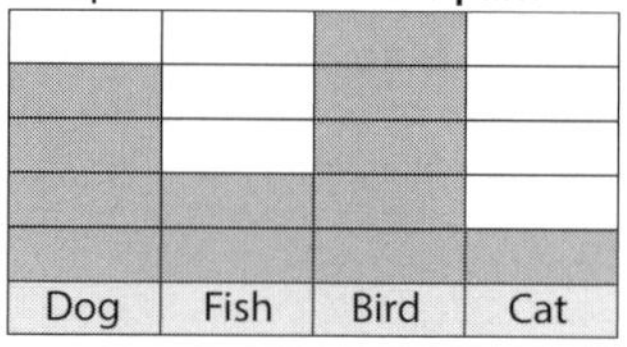

a 5 **b** 1 **c** 3 **d** 12

❸ **a** ■■□□ **b** ●●●●○○○○
c ▲▼▲▽△▽

13:3

7, 17, 27, 37, 47, 57, 67, 77, 87, 97

❶ 12, 13, 14, 15, 16, 17, 18, 19

10, 3, 4, 5, 6, 7, 8, 9

Half of each group of shapes will be coloured.
(2 triangles, 3 circles, 1 square will be coloured.)

14:1

5 groups of 3 = 15

❶ 2, 5, 8, 5, 4, 5 ❷ **a** 12 **b** 18 **c** 24

❸ 

❹ 5, 9, 13, 17, 21 ❺ an hour

❻ 6 groups of 2 = 12, 6 x 2 = 12

❼ 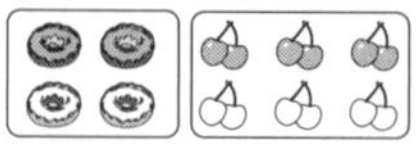
Half of each is coloured.

❽ **a** 23, 33, 43, 53, 63, 73 **b** 32, 42, 52, 62, 72, 82

❾ **a** 8 **b** 12 **c** 16 ❿ **a** 10 **b** 9

⓫ 4 + 4 = 8, 2 x 4 = 8 ⓬ 12, 13, 11, 14, 12

14:2

4 groups of 5 = 20

1 **a** 5 **b** 10 **c** 15 **d** 5 **e** 10 **f** 15

2 Answers may vary.

lives in trees	●	●	●				
lives on land	●	●	●	●	●		
lives in water	●	●	●	●	●		

3 4, 7, 10, 13, 16, 19 Rule: add 3

14:3

5 groups of 2 = 10

1 **a** 9 **b** 12 **c** 8 **d** 10 **e** 21 **f** 15 **g** 18 **h** 6

Half of each group of shapes will be coloured.
(4 triangles, 2 ovals, 6 squares will be coloured.)

15:1

4 groups of 4 = 16

1 23

2 

3 group of 2 flower will be drawn.
3 groups of 2 = 6
3 X 2 = 6

3 true 4 $1.10

5 **a**

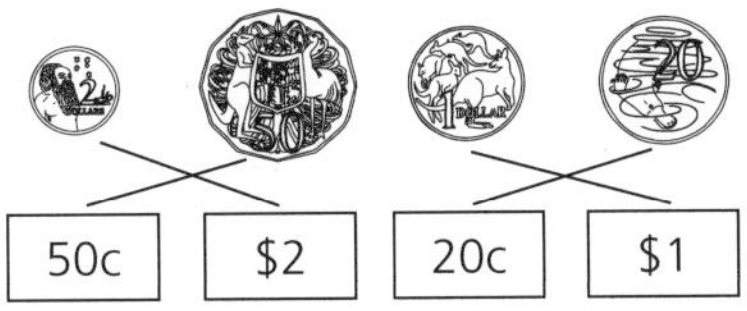

b The $2 and $1 coins will be coloured yellow.

6 8 (horns), 2 + 2 + 2 + 2 = 8

7 50 (cents)

8 10, 2 rows of 5 = 10, 2

9 

5 rows of 2 balls will be drawn.

10, yes

15:2

1 **a** 6, 6, 6 **b** 10, 10, 10 **c** 2, 4, 6, 8, 10, 12, 14, 16, 18

2 **a** 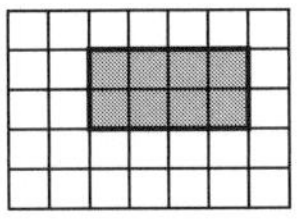

8, 8, 8, 8

b 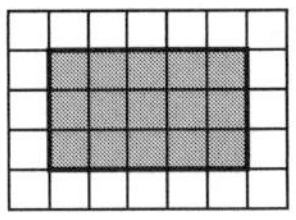

15, 15, 15, 15

c 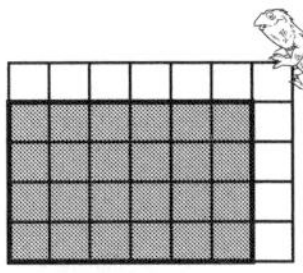

24, 24, 24, 24

15:3

18, 16, 14, 12, 10, 8, 6, 4, 2

1 **a** 2, 4, 6, 8, 10, 12, 14, 16

b 22, 24, 26, 28, 30, 32, 34

c 5, 10, 15, 20, 25, 30, 35

d 10, 20, 30, 40, 50, 60, 70

e 100, 110, 120, 130, 140, 150

10 groups of ten dots = 100

16:1

4 groups of 6 = 24

1 8 + 8 = 16, 16 2 $1.75

3 2, 4, 6, 8, 10, 12, 14

4 5 groups of 2 = 10, 5 x 2 = 10

5 79, 80

6 15, true 7 3, 6, 9, 12, 15, 18, 21

8 6, 2 rows of 3 = 6, 2 9 6, true

10 

11 quarter past 6 or 6 fifteen

12 3 groups of 8 cats = 24 cats altogether, 24

16:2

10 – 3 = 7

1 **a** 5, 10, 15, 20, 25, 30, 35, 40, 45, 50, 55, 60

b 3, 6, 9, 12, 15, 18, 21, 24, 27, 30, 33, 36

2 **a** 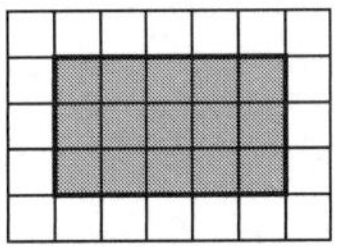

3 rows of 5 = 15

15, 15

b

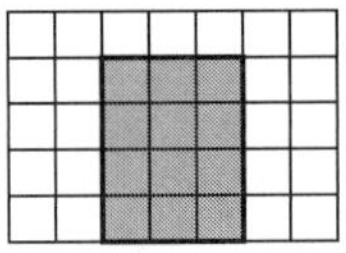

4 rows of 3 = 12

12, 12

c

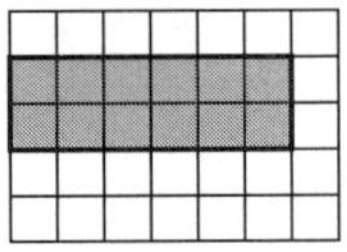

2 rows of 6 = 12

12, 12

❸ There will be 5 balls drawn in each box.15, 15

16:3

4 groups of 3 = 12

10, 20, 30, 40, 50, 60, 70, 80, 90

10, 20, 30, 40, 50, 60, 70, 80

40, 60, 90, 30, 70, 50, 80, 20

17:1

3 groups of 4 are shown.

❶ **a** 12 **b** 3 **c** 4 **d** 3 groups of 4 = 12
e yes

❷ 3 + 3 = 6, 2 x 3 = 6 ❸ $1.20

❹ 14, true ❺ 2, 4, 6, 8, 10, 12, 14

❻ 4 groups of 2 = 8, 4 x 2 = 8 ❼ 579

❽ **a** 753 **b** 625 **c** 292

❾ **a** 4 (paperclips) **b** 2 (paperclips)

17:2

6 groups of 1 = 6

❶ **a** 310 **b** 420 **c** 504 **d** 847 **e** 721

❷ **a** the plum **b** the ruler (or the peg)
c 6 (pegs) **d** 9 (pegs)

❸ 11, 14, 12, 15, 14

17:3

100, 200, 300, 400, 500, 600, 700

❶ 2, 14, 8, 16, 10, 18, 12, 6

0, 12, 18, 20, 14, 10, 16, 4

18:1

200, 201, 202, 203, 204, 205, 206

❶ **a** 218 **b** 139 **c** 537 **d** 392

❷ **a** 537 **b** 460

❸ 336, 519 ❹ **a** 5 **b** 3

❺ about the same

❻ 14, 18 ❼ 10, 14 ❽ 459 ❾ 369

❿

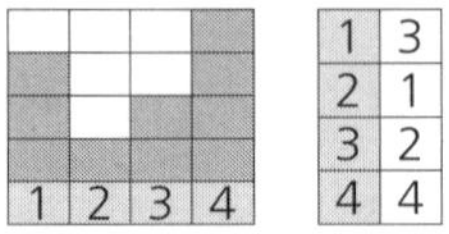

⓫ 12, 8, 4, 10, 6

18:2

10 + 10 = 20

❶ **a** 344 **b** 465 **c** 700 **d** 290
e 511 **f** 199

❷ 777 will be circled. 700, 707, 770, 777

❸ 12, 11, 15, 13, 14

18:3

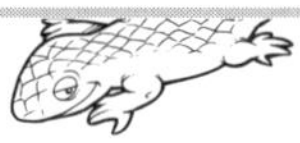

3 X 8 = 24

❶ **a** 6 (bolts) **b** 16 (bolts) **c** 12 (bolts)
d 60 (bolts) **e** 3 (globes) **f** 5 (globes)

80 camels

19:1

❶ **a** 111 **b** 104

❷ **a** 2, 4, 6, 8, 10 **b** 10, 8, 6, 4, 2
c 1, 3, 5, 7, 9 **d** 9, 7, 5, 3, 1
e 10, 20, 30, 40, 50
f 100, 200, 300, 400, 500

❸ **a** 152 **b** 491 **c** 375 **d** 573

❹ 713 will be circled. 293, 429, 501, 713

❺ 5 hundreds + 3 tens + 6 ones

❻ 24, 17

ISBN 978 0 6557 0882 7

7 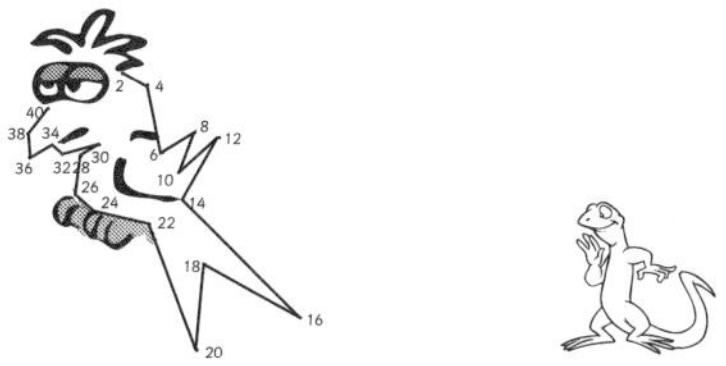

8 a The middle line will be traced over in red.

b The bottom line will be traced over in green.

9 641 10 327 11 10, 11, 11, 10, 12

19:2

1 5c, 10c, 20c, 50c, $1, $2

2 a

	Tally	Number
H	HHT HHT HHT I	16
T	HHT HHT IIII	14

b 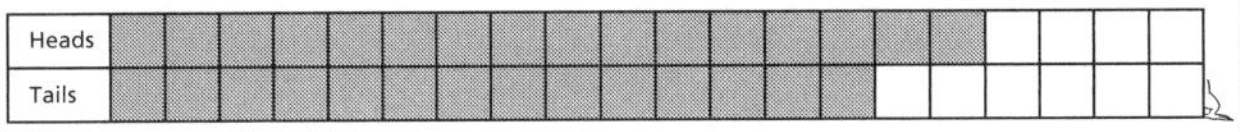

c heads

19:3

10, 20, 30, 40, 50, 60, 70, 80

1 a 1, 3, 5, 7, 9 2, 4, 6, 8, 10

b 5, 10, 15, 20, 25 50, 45, 40, 35, 30

c 19, 17, 15, 13, 11 20, 18, 16, 14, 12

10 sheep, 10 lizards

20:1

5, 15, 25, 35, 45, 55, 65, 75

1 129, 112 2 953 3 462 4 9

5 a 21 b 31 6 Answers will vary.

7 a 12, 14, 16, 18, 20

b 5, 10, 15, 20, 25

c 7, 9, 11, 13, 15

d 30, 25, 20, 15, 10

8 221 9 682 will be circled. 199, 400, 509, 682

10 16 (triangles), 18 (rhombuses)

11 12, 14, 13, 13, 13

20:2

13, 23, 33, 43, 53, 63, 73, 83

1 a 53 tens 8 ones b 82 tens 9 ones

c 45 d 52

2 a 9 + 15 = 24 and 9 + 25 = 34

b 6 + 15 = 21 and 6 + 25 = 31

3 a 120 b 132 c 128

4 a 116 b 129 c 102

5 16, 16, 18, 14, 16

20:3

18, 28, 38, 48, 58, 68, 78, 88

1 a 14 – 11 = 3 b 3 groups of 4 = 12

2 a and b Answers will vary.

18 groups of 2 balls = 36

21:1

4, 14, 24, 34, 44, 54, 64, 74

1 8, 8, 5, 3

2 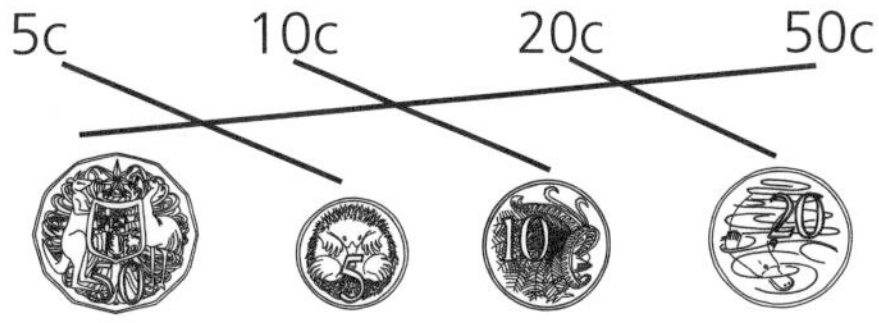

3 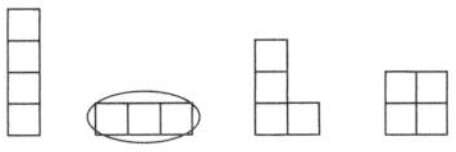

4 a 22 b 32 5 8 + 8 = 16

6 This is called a number line. 7 12 (squares)

8 Answers will vary. 10 complete squares will be coloured to make a shape.

9 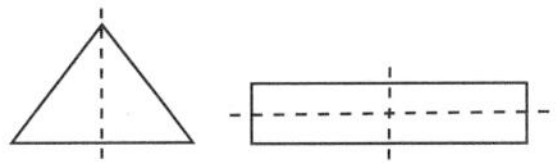

10 The oval will be circled. 11 9, 9, 10, 11, 11

21:2

6 (triangles)

1 one dollar fifty cents twenty cents two dollars

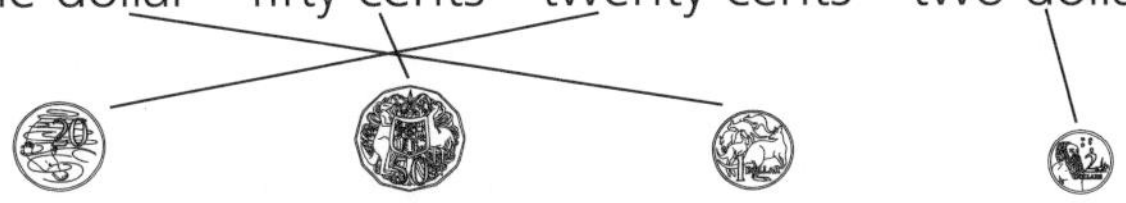

2 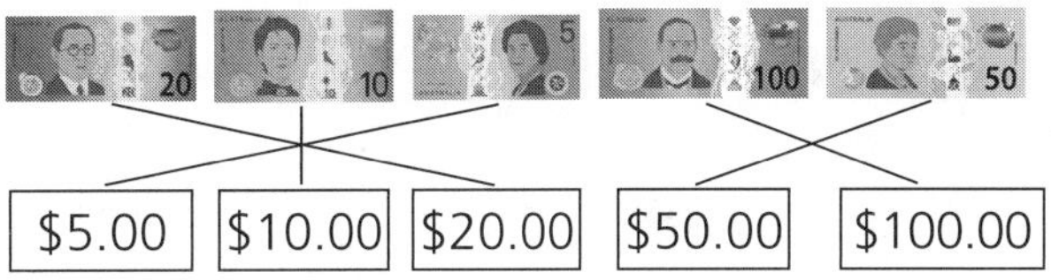

3 8, 7, 5, 9, 6

21:3

30, 35, 40, 45, 50, 55, 60, 65, 70, 75

1 **a** 17 **b** 21 **c** 12 **d** 21 **e** 14 **f** 16 **g** 23 **h** 24

 10 pelicans,  26 pumas,

 12 paw prints

22:1

$3.85

1 **a** 3 **b** 7 **2** **a** 12 **b** 30

3 53 tens 4 ones

4 **a** 41 **b** 52 **5** 3 rows of 6 = 18

6 Answers will vary.

7 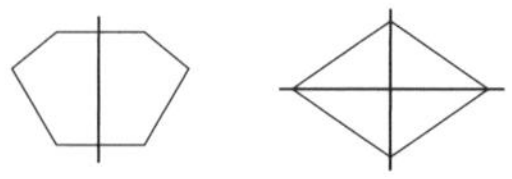 **8** $1.80 **9** $20, $50

10

127	179	100	172
170	180	189	170

11 **a** 422 **b** 894 **12** 40c

13 13, 13, 15, 15, 17

22:2

10 (squares)

1 The 5c and 10c coins will be circled. The 50c, 5c, 10c and 20c coins will be coloured grey. The $1 coin will be coloured yellow. $1.85 altogether

2 **A** 3 (units), **B** 6 (units), **C** 4 (units), **D** 6 (units), **E** 5 (units) Shapes B and D will be coloured.

3 **a** 39 tens 2 ones **b** 54 tens 3 ones **c** 38 **d** 72

22:3

$5, $10, $20, $50 and $100 notes are shown.

1 **a** 

b 

 16 mice,  16 lobsters,  12 ostriches

23:1

$1.40, $1.10, $1.05

1 **a** 5 **b** 8 **2** **a** 10 **b** 50

3 25 tens 7 ones **4** **a** 16 **b** 42 **c** 83 **d** 10

5 Cone, curved, rolls, flat and slides will be circled.

6  5 (groups of 5), 25 (altogether)

7 56 tens 7 ones **8** 80c

9 (5c) (5c) (5c) (5c)

10 

11  3 (surfaces)
2 (flat surfaces)
1 (curved surface)

12 **a** 12 **b** 3 **c** 4 **13** 7, 10, 19, 6, 9

23:2

$3.85

1 

2 **a** 20 **b** 4 **c** 5

3 One flat surface on each 3D object will be shaded.

4 16, 19, 17, 18, 20

23:3

3 groups of 2 = 6

1 **a** 95c **b** $1.90 **c** $1.85 **d** $2.45

24:1

3 groups of 2 = 6

1 **a** 19 + 4 = 19 + 1 + 3 = 23

b 18 + 3 = 18 + 2 + 1 = 21

c 19 + 5 = 24

2 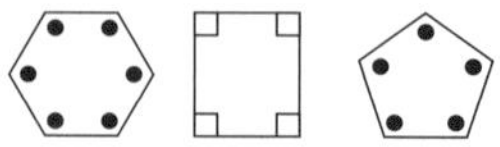

3 $1.30 **4** **a** 8 **b** 2 **c** 4

 ISBN 978 0 6557 0882 7

5  2 (surfaces), 1 (flat surface), 1 (curved surface)

6 9

7 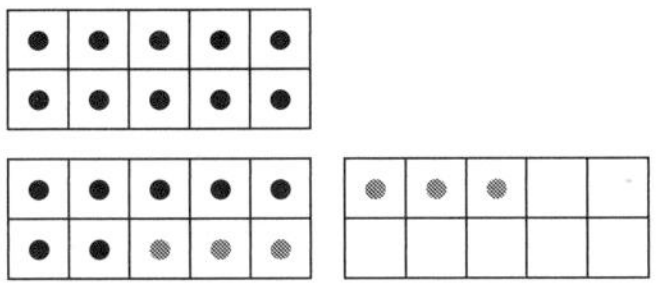

The grey dots will be drawn.

$17 + 6 = 17 + 3 + 3$
$= 20 + 3$
$= 23$

8 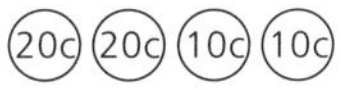

9 cylinder

24:2

cylinder, cube, cone, prism, pyramid, prism, pyramid

1 Answers will vary. One flat surface will be coloured on each object.

2 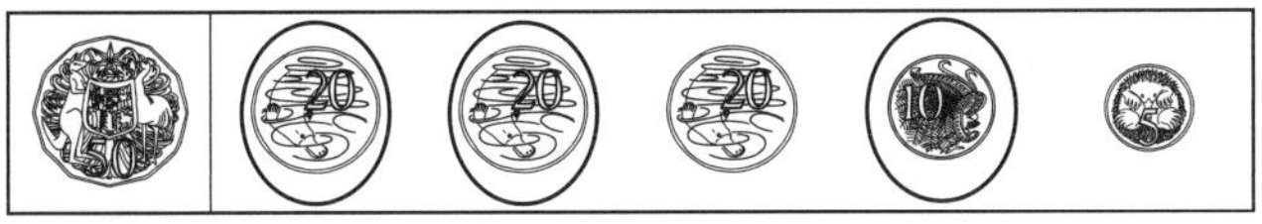

3

+	7	5	8	6	9	4
3	10	8	11	9	12	7
5	12	10	13	11	14	9

	10	7	9	5	8	6
−5	5	2	4	0	3	1
−3	7	4	6	2	5	3

4 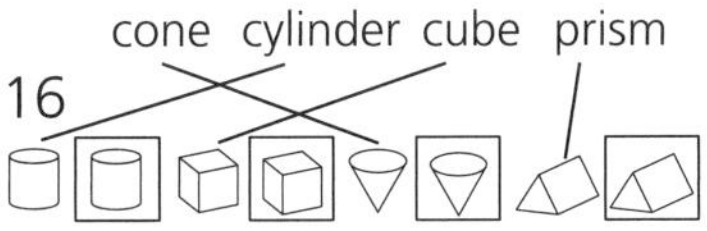

5 17, 13, 17, 19, 16

24:3

30c, 25c, 30c

1 **a** 50c **b** 55c **c** 35c **d** 45c
e 80c **f** 90c

 45 tortoises

25:1

<u>6</u> + <u>7</u> = <u>13</u>

1 1, 3, 2, 4

2 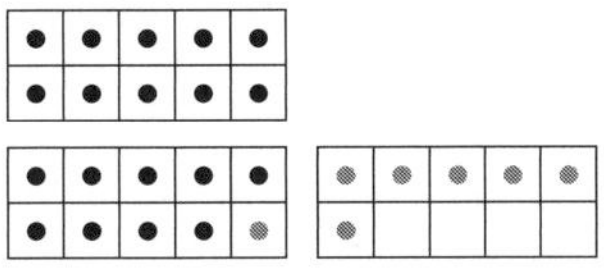

$19 + 7 = 19 + 1 + 6$
$= 20 + 6$
$= 26$

3 33, 43, 55, 63

4 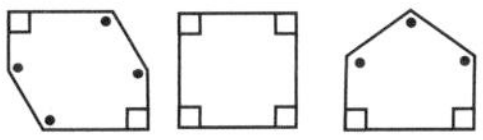

5 5

6 The teddy will be circled.

7 90, 80, 9, 9

8 87, 95, 38, 38

9 Table:

yes	2
no	4

Graph:

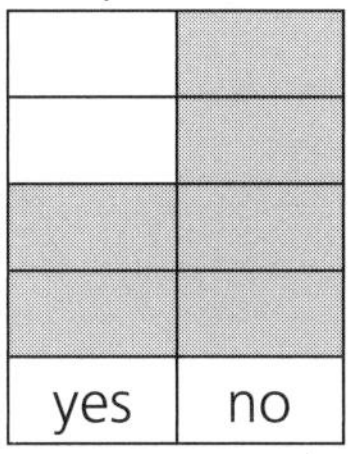

10 9, 9, 9, 9, 10

25:2

21, 31, 41, <u>51</u>, <u>61</u>, <u>71</u>, <u>81</u>, <u>91</u>

1 **a** 432, four hundred and thirty-two
b 294, two hundred and ninety-four
c 705, seven hundred and five

2 12, 12, 15, 14, 14

25:3

145, 146, 147, <u>148</u>, <u>149</u>, <u>150</u>, <u>151</u>, <u>152</u>

1

7	
1	<u>6</u>
<u>3</u>	4
6	<u>1</u>
5	<u>2</u>
2	<u>5</u>
4	<u>3</u>

8	
<u>1</u>	7
4	<u>4</u>
<u>7</u>	1
2	<u>6</u>
<u>5</u>	3
6	<u>2</u>
<u>3</u>	5

9	
<u>1</u>	8
6	<u>3</u>
2	<u>7</u>
<u>4</u>	5
<u>8</u>	1
3	<u>6</u>
7	<u>2</u>
<u>5</u>	4

10	
<u>1</u>	9
6	<u>4</u>
<u>3</u>	7
4	<u>6</u>
<u>5</u>	5
2	<u>8</u>
<u>7</u>	3
8	<u>2</u>
1	<u>9</u>

26:1

6, 8, 7

1 54, 73, 264, 143, 352, 432

2 85, 97, 39, 99, 77, 98

3 **a** 8 **b** 4 **c** 9 **d** 6

4 **a** 5 **b** 2 **c** 8 **d** 7

5 **a** 20 **b** 21 **c** 34 **d** 35 **e** 97 **f** 84

6 50, 50, 90, 90

7 greater

8 3, 0

9 The last triangle will be coloured.

10 Answers will vary. One answer could be 'an apple'.

26:2

145, 146, 147, <u>148</u>, <u>149</u>, <u>150</u>, <u>151</u>, <u>152</u>, <u>153</u>

1 **a** 2 **b** 4 **2** 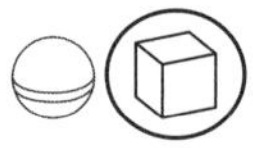 **3** 75, 85, 97

4 **a** 9 **b** 8

5 <u>3</u> hundreds <u>6</u> tens <u>2</u> ones

6 10, 10, 10, 10, 10

26:3

134, 133, 132, <u>131</u>, <u>130</u>, <u>129</u>, <u>128</u>, <u>127</u>, <u>126</u>

1 **a**

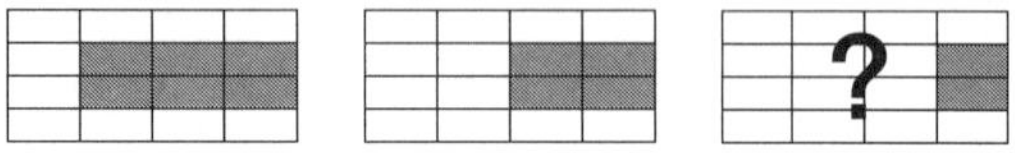

<u>6</u> grey tiles <u>10</u> white tiles — <u>4</u> grey tiles <u>12</u> white tiles — <u>2</u> grey tiles <u>14</u> white tiles

b 20 grey tiles **c** 44 white tiles

 62 elephants

27:1

6

1 63, 93, 364, 854 **2** 3, Each has <u>3</u>.

3

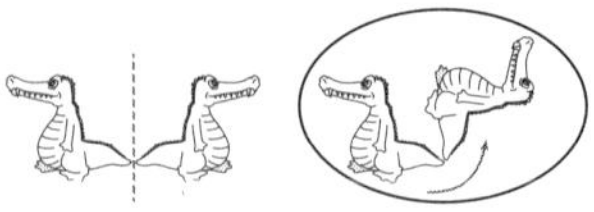

4

5 **a** 7 **b** 5 **c** 3 **d** 8

6 **a** 1 **b** 2 **c** 9 **d** 6

7 87, 98, 89, 85 **8** **a** 6, 6 **b** 4, 4 **c** 2, 2

9 4, 3

10

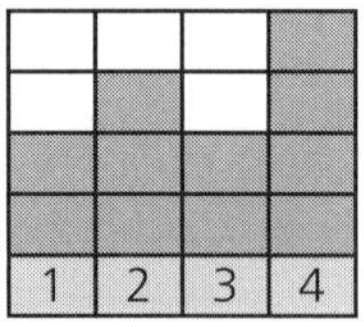

1	2
2	3
3	2
4	4

27:2

3 groups of <u>4</u> = <u>12</u>

1 **a** 2, 2 **b** 6, 6 **c** 3, 3 **d** 4, 4 **e** 1, 1

2 **a** 4, 12, 8 **b** 12, 15, 16

3 12, 8, 4, 10, 6

27:3

16

1

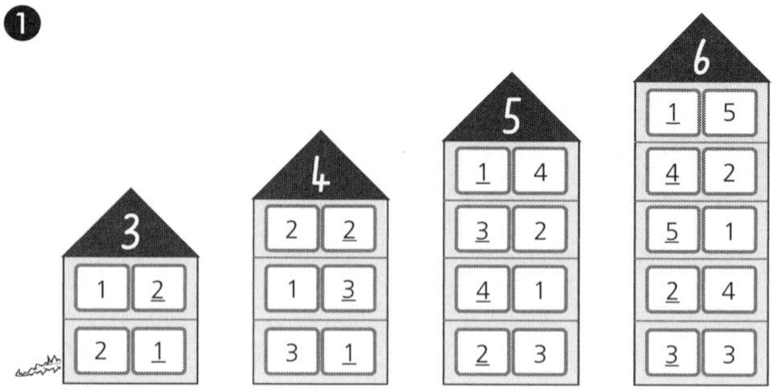

28:1

9

1 32, 46, 53, 43 **2** 56, 74 **3** 4, Each has <u>4</u>.

4 13 **5** 92,

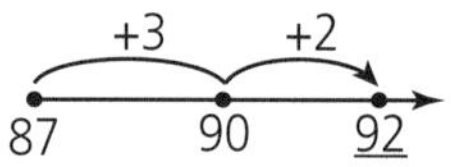

6 88,

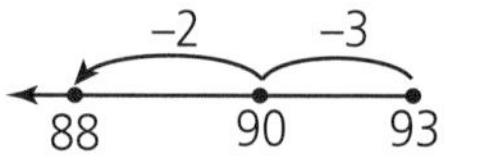

7 2, Each has <u>2</u>. **8** **a** 15 **b** 5, 5 **c** 3, 3

9 **a** 537 **b** 460

10

d	卌 卌 |
f	卌 卌

d was used more.

28:2

4 groups of <u>2</u> = <u>8</u>

1 **a** 53,

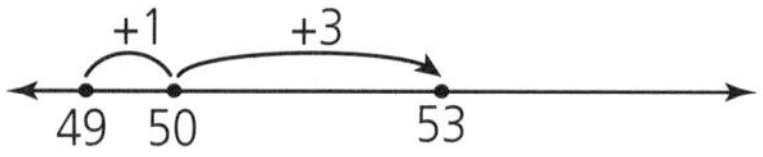

b 93,

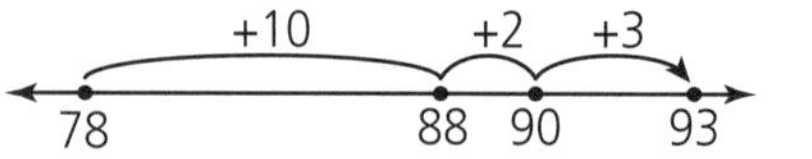

c 48,

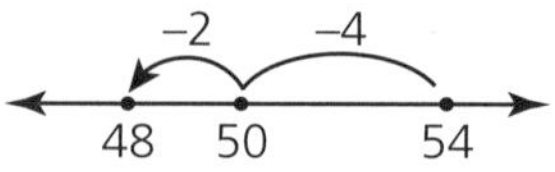

d 64,

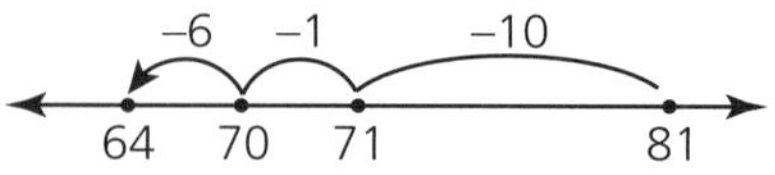

2 **a** F **b** C **c** B

3 <u>5</u> hundreds <u>7</u> tens <u>6</u> ones

4 14, 17, 13, 19, 16

 ISBN 978 0 6557 0882 7

28:3

To add 9, you can add 10 first then take away 1.

❶ 12, 13, 14, 15, 16, 17, 18, 19   10, 3, 4, 5, 6, 7, 8, 9

29:1

127, 128, 129, 130, 131, 132, 133

❶ 80,
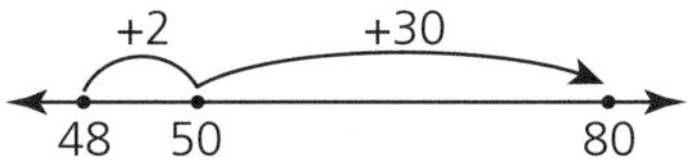

❷ 36,
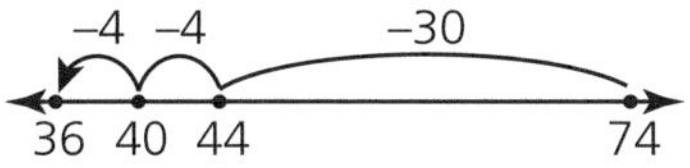

❸ 24 ❹

❺ a
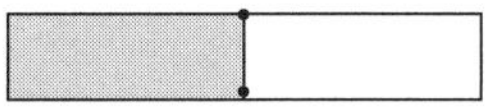
b

❻ 3, Each has 3 cans.

❼ a 43 tens 6 ones b 38 tens 6 ones

❽ a 14 b 24

❾ a 10, 10 b 5, 5 c 4, 4 ❿ 17

29:2

28 (eagles)

❶ 4, 6, 8 ❷ 5 ❸

A			
	B		

❸

❹ 18, 16, 14, 12, 10

29:3

❶ a park b beach c home d pool e beach

30:1

❶ 73,
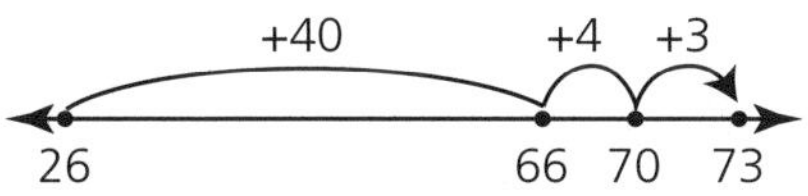

❷ 57,
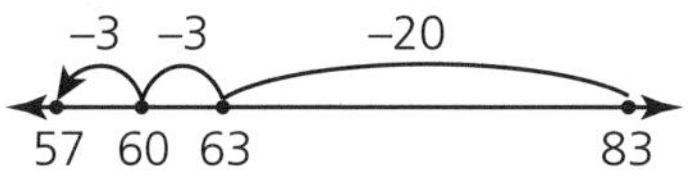

❸ 5 group of 2 = 10, 10, 10

❹ a
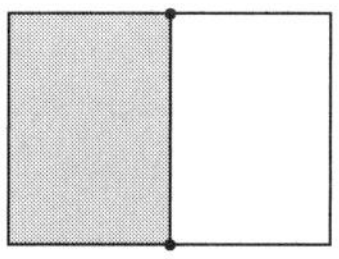
b
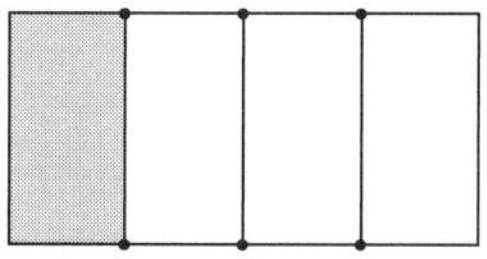

❺ 12 (months)

❻ September, October, November

❼ June, July August

❽ 6 (months)

❾ a 218 b 139 c 537 d 392

❿

8 cupcakes will be circled.
4 cupcakes will be coloured.

30:2

3 groups of 4 = 12

❶
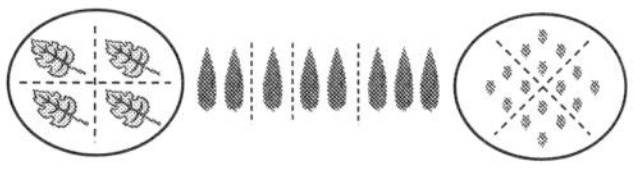

❷ a

b 4 c 8

d
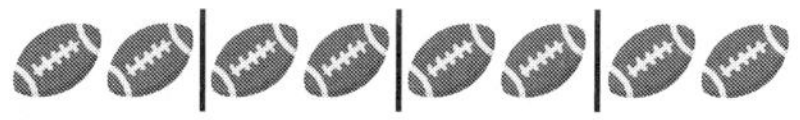
e 2

❸ a 53 b 95 c 57

❹ a 51,
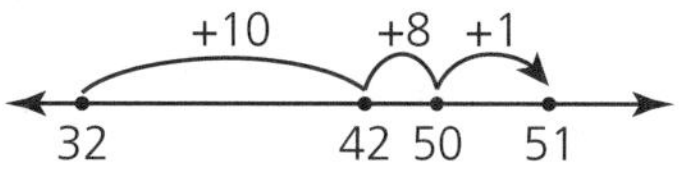

b 38,
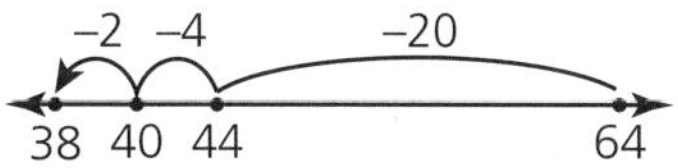

30:3

5, 10, 9

❶ a picture graph, pie graph b yes
c Answers will vary.

31:1

❶ 14, 16, 14, 15 ❷ 366

❸ a

b 2

c

d 1

❹ a 9 b 15 c 21 ❺ 5

 • *AUSTRALIAN SIGNPOST MATHS 2 MENTALS* • ISBN 978 0 6557 0882 7

❻ Answers will vary. A shape with parallel lines will be drawn, e.g. a square, rectangle or trapezium.

❼ The 2D shapes will be traced. The shapes are rectangle, square, rhombus or diamond, trapezium. All shapes have 4 sides and 4 vertices.

❽ 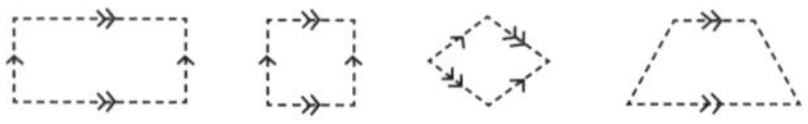

❾ 12 (months)

❿ The word 'quarter' will be circled. ⓫ 2

⓬ 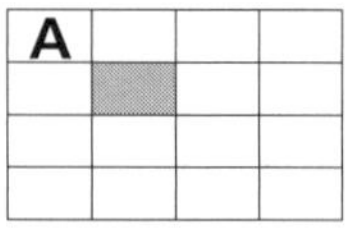

⓭ 11, 13, 17, 15, 13

31:2

3, 6, 9, 12, 15, 18, 21, 24, 27

❶ a OOOOOO|OOOOOO b 6 c 12

d OOO|OOO|OOO|OOO e 3

❷ a 2 (months) 5 (days) b 2 (months) 16 (days)

c 4 (months) 6 (days)

❸ a 75 b 79 c 76

31:3

1st, 2nd, 3rd, 4th, 5th, 6th, 7th

❶ HID, DAYS, OLD, SLID

32:1

4, 8, 12, 14

❶ 10, 5, 16, 8, 8, 4, 14, 7 ❷ 2, 10, 20, 6 ❸ 80c

❹ 12 ❺ 6, 3 groups of 2 = 6 ❻ 3 ❼ 6

❽ The rectangle will be circled.

❾ The word 'doubles' will be circled.

❿ 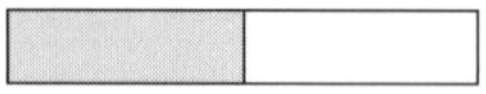 ⓫ 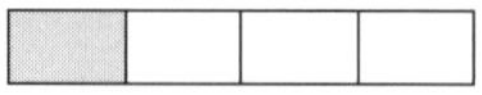

⓬ 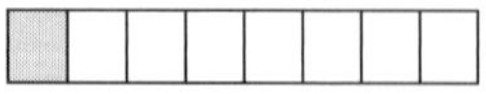 ⓭ 4 ⓮ 3 (towers)

32:2

❶ a August 18th b August 16th c 24 (months)

❷ 

❸ a 4 (giraffes) b 3 (elephants)

❹ a E b D c F d H

32:3

2, 10, 20, 12

❶ 2, 14, 8, 16, 10, 18, 12, 6

0, 12, 18, 20, 14, 10, 16, 4

33:1

18, 16, 14, 12, 10, 8, 6, 4, 2

❶ 4, 6, 8 ❷ 60c ❸ 3, 6

❹ 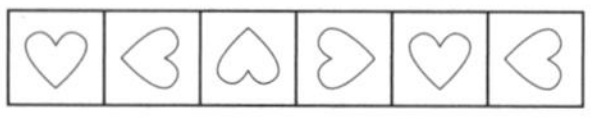

❺ One small rectangle will be coloured.

❻ The word 'half' will be circled.

❼ 4, 2, 12, 6, 6, 3, 18, 9

❽ 90, 80, 70, 60, 50, 40 2, 4, 6, 8, 10, 12

95, 90, 85, 80, 75, 70 13, 23, 33, 43, 53, 63

30, 35, 40, 45, 50, 55

❾ 10 ❿ The word 'halves' will be circled.

⓫ 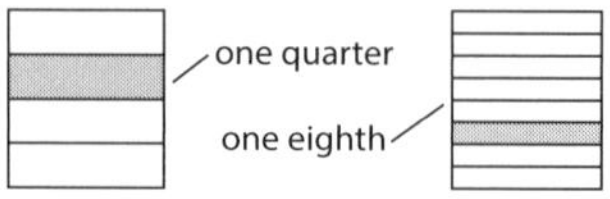

⓬ 10, 12, 14, 16, 18

33:2

31, 36, 41, 46, 51, 56, 61, 66, 71, 76

❶ a 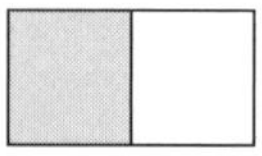 b 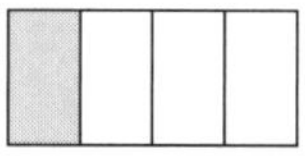 c 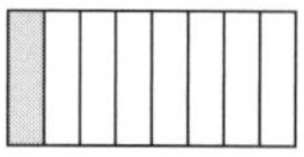

❷ a 26th July b 8th July c 62 (days)

❸ 9, 19, 29, 39, 49, 59, 69, 79, 89, 99, 109

209, 219, 229, 239, 249, 259, 269, 279, 289, 299

33:3

2 groups of 3 = 6

❶ a 100, 98, 96, 94, 92 ,90, 88

b 100, 90, 80, 70, 60, 50, 40

c 100, 95, 90, 85, 80, 75, 70

  • *AUSTRALIAN SIGNPOST MATHS 2 MENTALS* • ISBN 978 0 6557 0882 7

d 79, 77, 75, 73, 71, 69, 67, 65, 63

e 89, 79, 69, 59, 49, 39, 29, 19, 9

8 groups of ten dogs = 80

34:1

❶ 24, 31 ❷ 15, 38, 16, 54

❸ a 79,

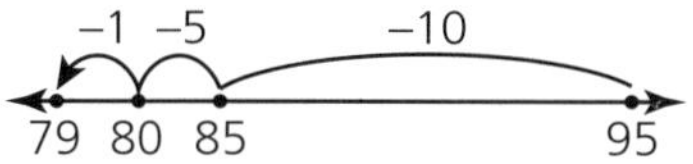

b 92,

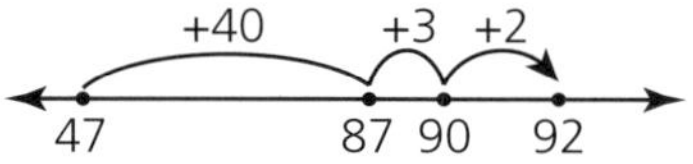

❹ 4, 8

❺ a 67 b 82 c 99 d 91 e 68 f 100

❻

❼ a

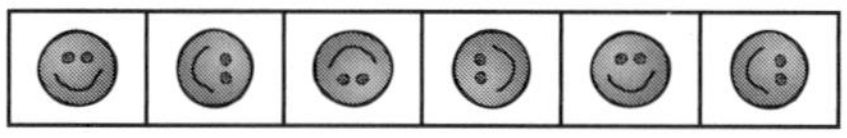

b This pattern is made using quarter turns.

❽ a 75, 70, 65, 60, 55, 50
b 55, 50, 45, 40, 35, 30
c 42, 44, 46, 48, 50, 52
d 80, 70, 60, 50, 40, 30
e 34, 44, 54, 64, 74, 84
f 124, 134, 144, 154, 164

❾ cube ❿ a 363 b 719 c 814 d 697
e 166 f 465 g 200 h 299

⓫ 8, 14, 11, 9, 12

34:2

cylinder, cube, cone, prism, pyramid, prism, pyramid

❶

	Number of faces	Number of edges	Number of vertices	Number of curved surfaces	Number of flat surfaces
cylinder	0	2	0	1	2
cube	6	12	8	0	6

❷ 5, 15, 25, 35, 45, 55, 65, 75, 85, 95, 105

605, 615, 625, 635, 645, 655, 665, 675, 685, 695

7, 17, 27, 37, 47, 57, 67, 77, 87, 97, 107

207, 217, 227, 237, 247, 257, 267, 277, 287, 297

❸ a 63

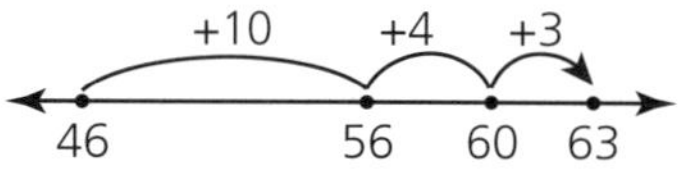

b 15,

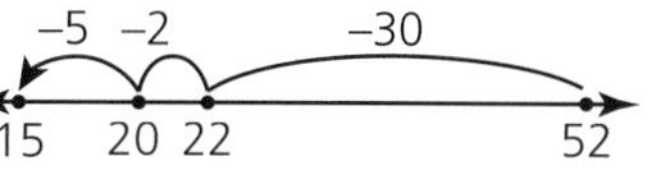

❹ 13, 15, 16, 14, 12

34:3

25, 12

❶

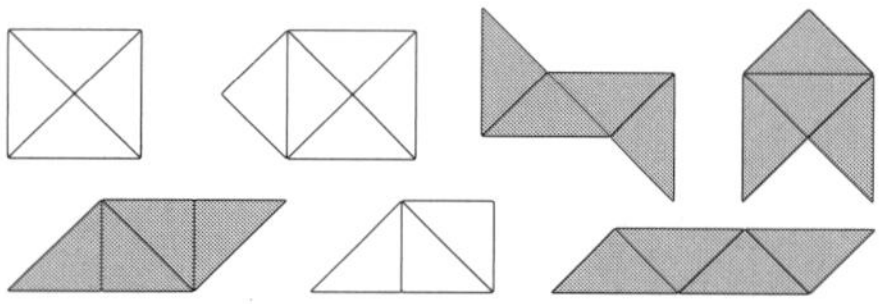

The 4 darker shapes will be coloured.

35:1

❶ 43, 62, 73, 31 ❷ 98, 40, 15, 92, 90, 44

❸ 17,

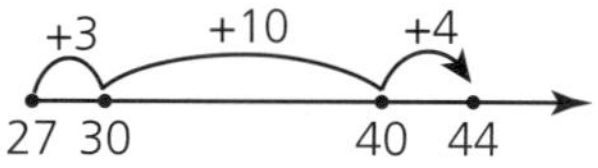

❹ 7 + 6 = 13, 6 + 7 = 13, 10 + 3 = 13

❺ 60, 58, 56, 54, 52, 50

❻ a 3 + 2 = 5 b 2 + 1 = 3 c 6 + 5 = 11

❼ 2 + 4 + 4 = 10, 4 + 4 + 2 = 10

❽ 12 + 1 + 7 = 20, 10 + 8 + 4 = 22, 17 + 5 + 2 = 24,

19 + 3 + 5 = 27

❾ 59, 71, 43, 37 ❿ a $50 b $65

⓫ 18, 12, 15, 17, 20

35:2

cone, prism, cylinder, sphere, prism, prism, pyramid

❶

	Number of faces	Number of edges	Number of vertices	Number of curved surfaces	Number of flat surfaces
	0	0	0	1	0
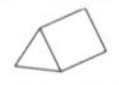	5	9	6	0	5

❷ a 98 b 86 c 93

❸ a 63,

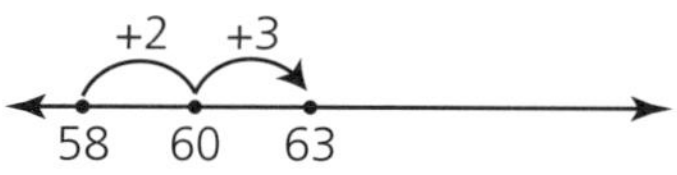

b 76,

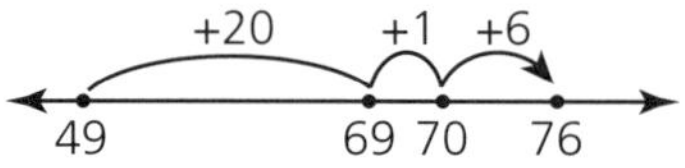

c 36,

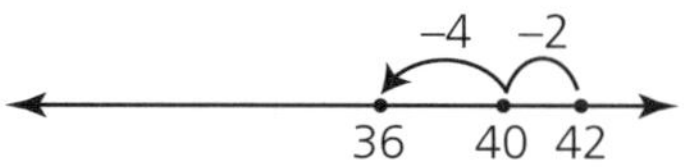

d 37,

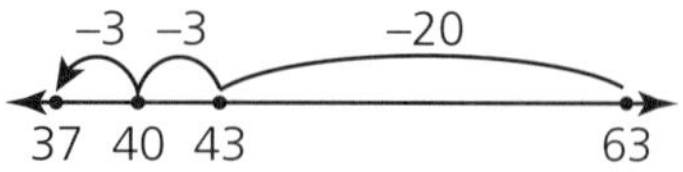

35:3

614, 624, 634, <u>644</u>, <u>654</u>, <u>664</u>, <u>674</u>, <u>684</u>

❶

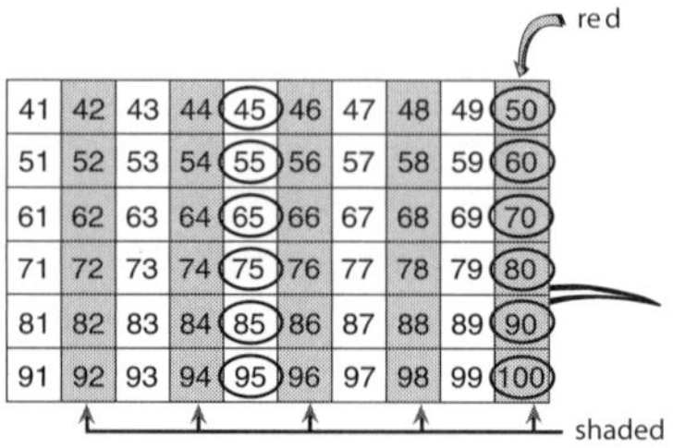

Multiple-choice questions

❶ 41

❷ 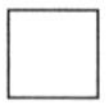

❸ 2

❹ 3 groups of 4

❺ 15

❻ 6

❼ above the bird

❽ 29

❾ D

❿ 11

Problem-solving challenge

❶ $1.30 ❷ 15 (people) ❸ $1.60

❹ **a** 27 **b** 104

❺ **a** 8 **b** 20 **c** Answers will vary.

❻ 5 (bracelets)

❼ **a** 3 (pentagons) **b** 17

❽ 110 minutes (or 1 hour 50 minutes)

❾ 14 (balls)

❿ 8 ($5 notes) ⓫ 18 (biscuits) ⓬ 70 (pages)

⓭ 2 (strawberries)

17:2

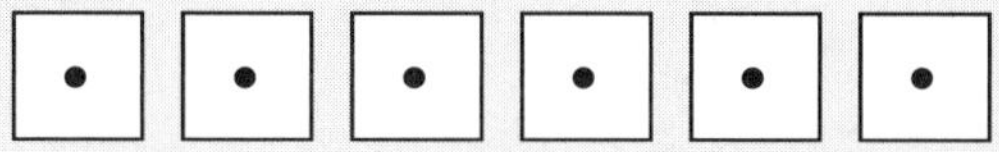 _____ groups of _____ = _____

❶ Write the numbers modelled.

a 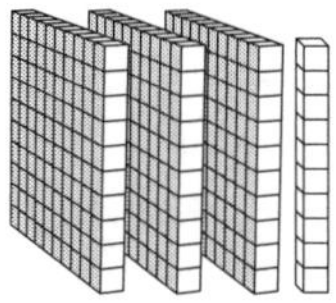 _____

b 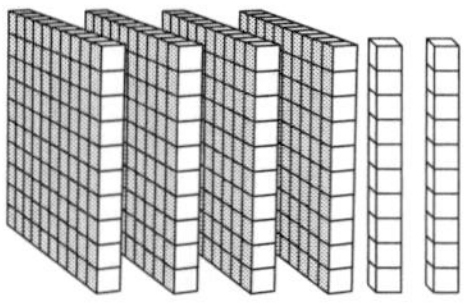 _____

c 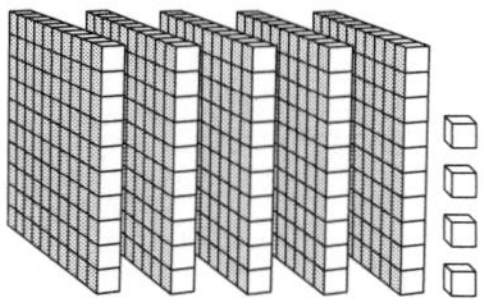 _____

d 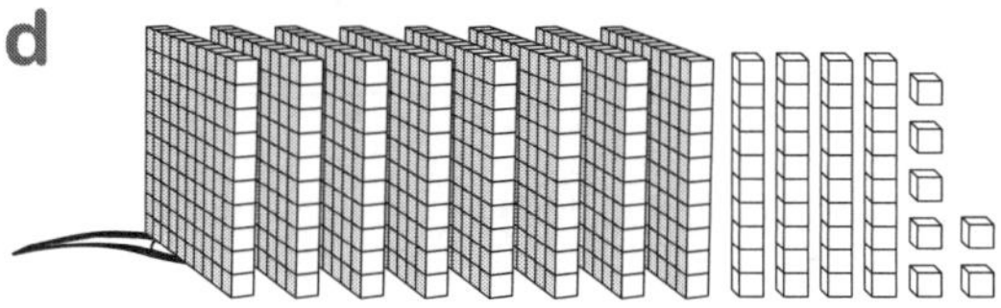 _____

e 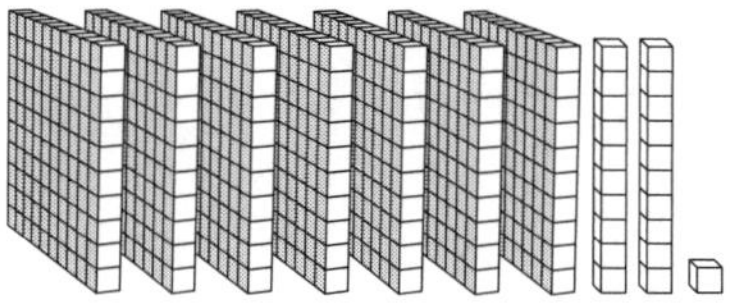 _____

❷ The ruler weighs the same as 2 pegs.
The pencil weighs the same as 3 pegs.
The plum weighs the same as 12 pegs.

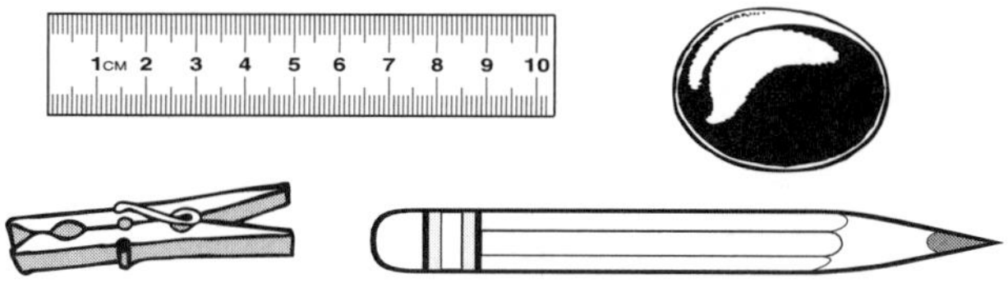

a Which is the heaviest? _______________

b Which is the lightest? _______________

c Two pencils weigh _____ pegs.

d Three pencils weigh _____ pegs.

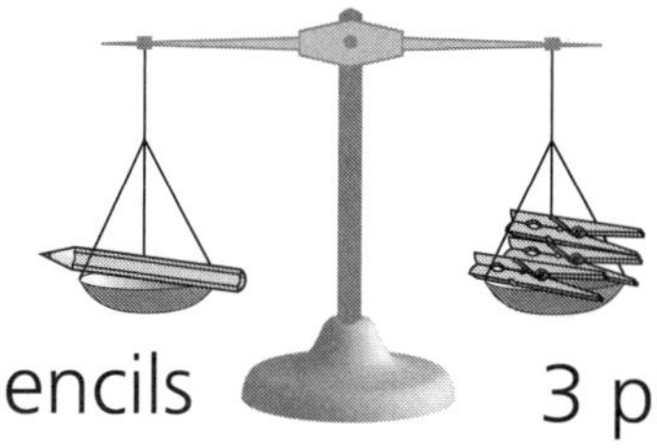

❸ 7 + 4 ☐ 9 + 5 ☐ 6 + 6 ☐ 9 + 6 ☐ 7 + 7 ☐

17:3

100, 200, 300, _____, _____, _____, _____

❶ Complete each number web.

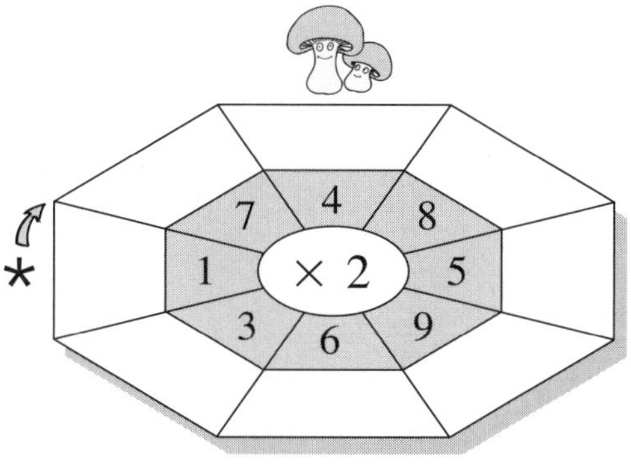

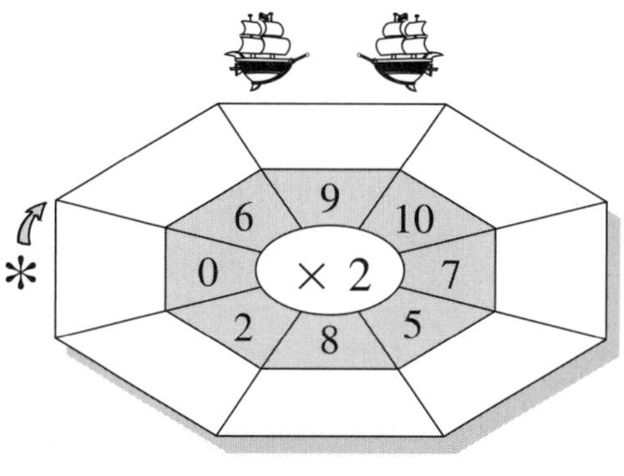

200, 201, 202, ______, 204, ______, ______

❶ Write the number after:

a 217 ______ b 138 ______

c 536 ______ d 391 ______

❷ Write the number before:

a 538 ______ b 461 ______

❸

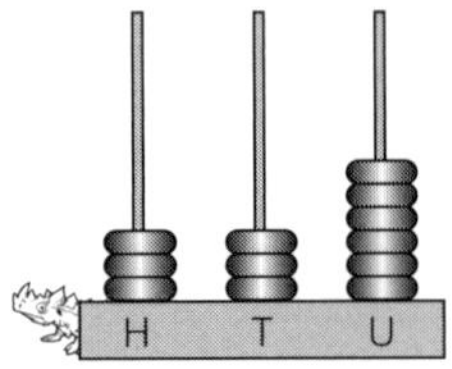

______

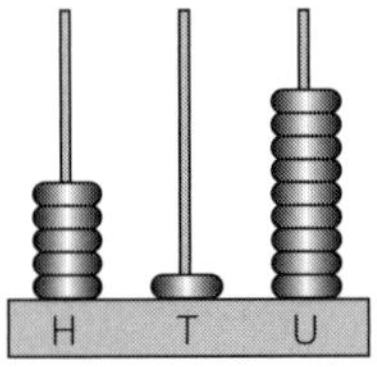

______

❹

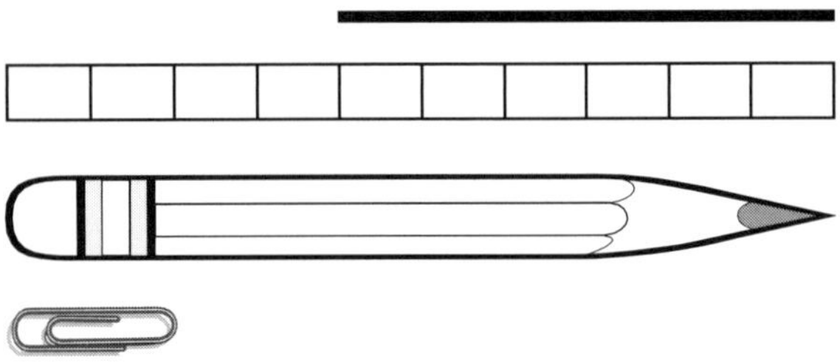

How many paperclips are the same length as:

a the pencil? ______

b the black line? ______

❺ Is the width of a door less than, about the same as, or more than one metre?

______

❻ 14 + 5 – 5 = ______

18 – 8 + 8 = ______

❼ 15 take away 5. ______

18 minus 4. ______

❽ Write the number modelled.

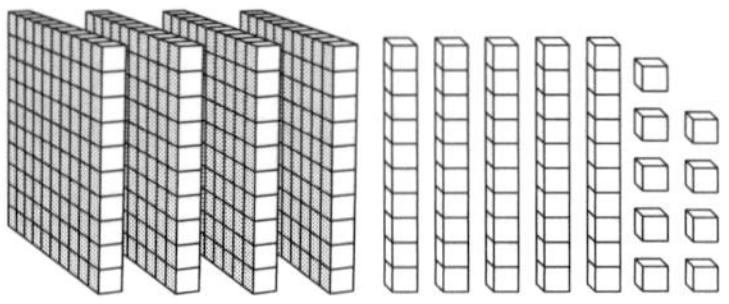

______

❾ 3 hundreds + 6 tens + 9 ones

= ______

❿ Use this list to complete the graph and table.

List

1, 4, 2, 3, 4, 1, 4, 3, 4, 1

Graph

1	2	3	4

Table

1	
2	
3	
4	

⓫ 6 + 6 ☐ 4 + 4 ☐ 2 + 2 ☐ 5 + 5 ☐ 3 + 3 ☐

18:2

 ☐ + ☐ = ☐

❶ Write each number shown.

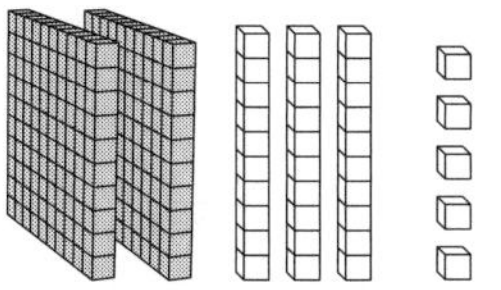

200 | 30 | 5 = 235

a 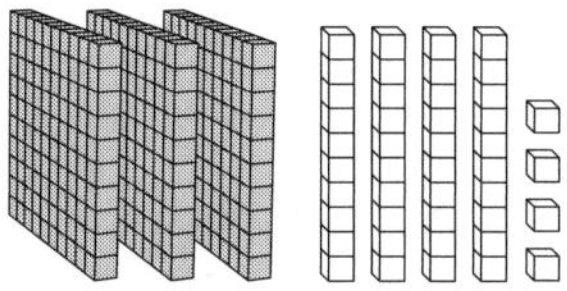 ______

b 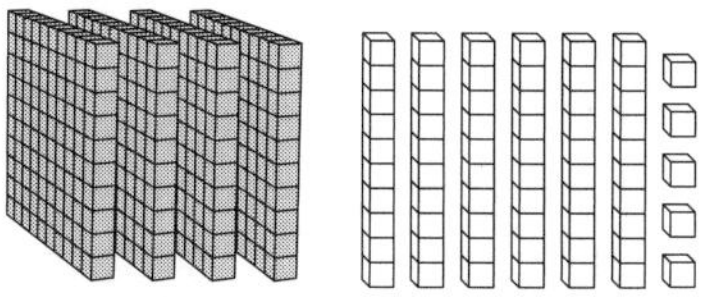 ______

c 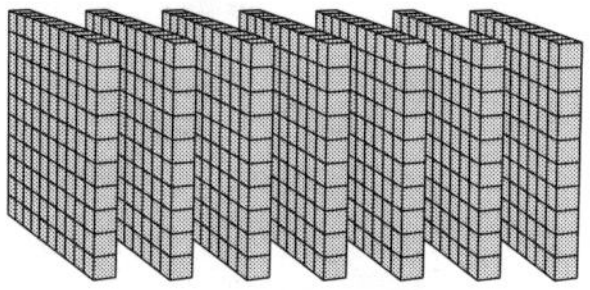 ______

d 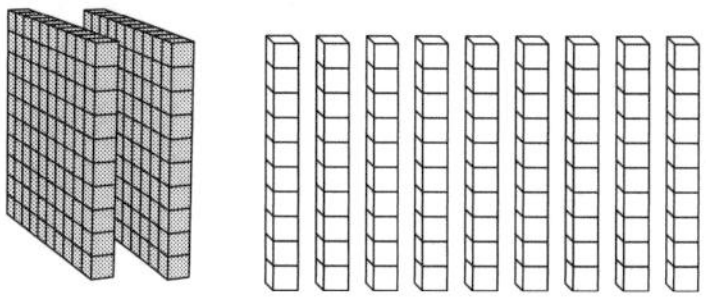 ______

e 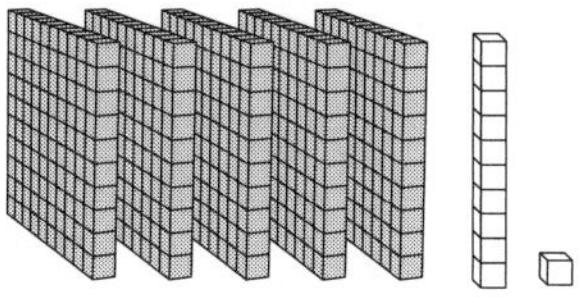 ______

f 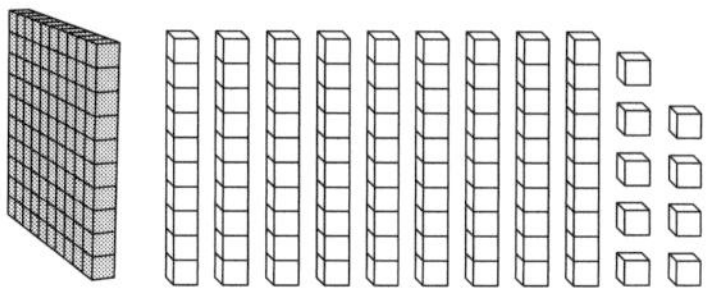 ______

❷ Circle the largest number: 707 770 777 700

Write the numbers in order from smallest to largest. ______

❸ 10 + 2 ☐ 10 + 1 ☐ 10 + 5 ☐ 10 + 3 ☐ 10 + 4 ☐

18:3

 , ☐ × ☐ = ☐

❶ How many bolts will balance:

a a globe and a lock? ______

b a torch and a candle? ______

c two candles? ______

d six torches? ______

How many globes will balance:

e a candle? ______

f a torch? ______

We balanced each object with bolts.

2 bolts

4 bolts

6 bolts

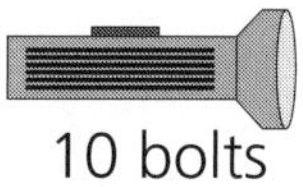

10 bolts

How many camels? ☐

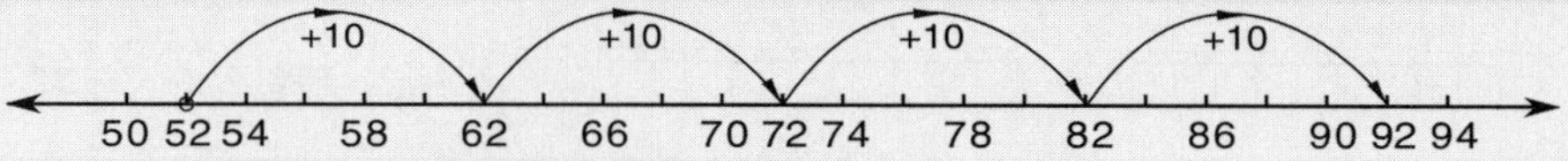

1

a 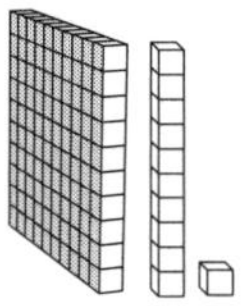 ______

b 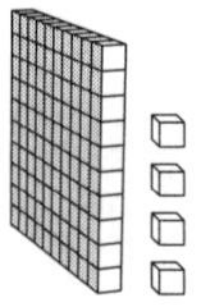 ______

2

a 2, 4, ______, 8, ______

b 10, 8, ______, ______, 2

c 1, 3, ______, ______, 9

d 9, 7, ______, ______, 1

e 10, 20, 30, ______, ______

f 100, 200, 300, ______, ______

3 Write the number before:

a 153 ______ b 492 ______

c 376 ______ d 574 ______

4 Circle the largest number and write the numbers in order.

293 501 429 713

____

5 536 = ______ hundreds + ______ tens + ______ ones

6 24 + 6 – 6 = ______

17 – 5 + 5 = ______

7 Join the dots counting by twos.

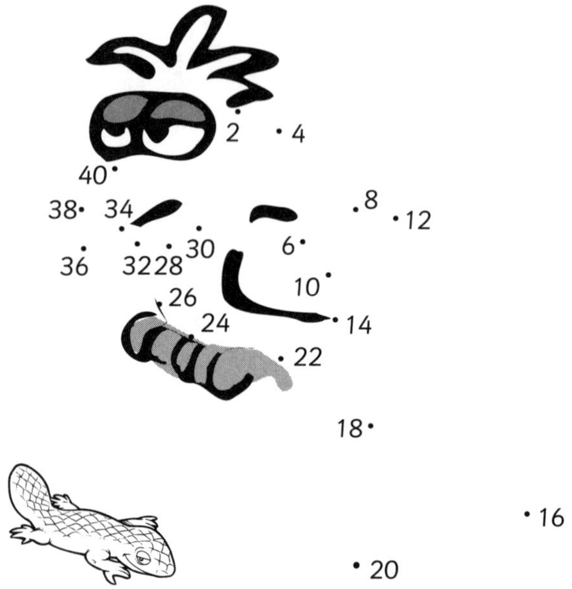

8

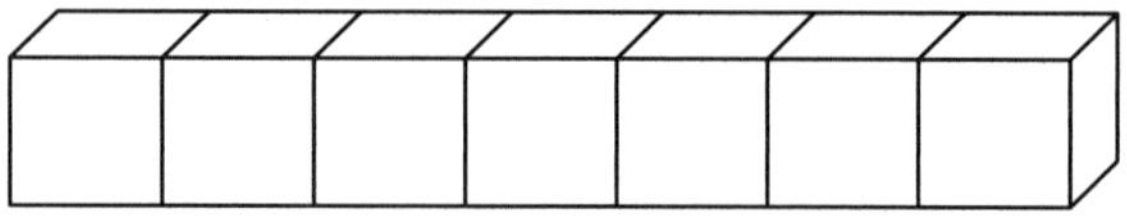

a Trace in red the line that is 3 ones blocks long.

b Trace in green the line that is 5 ones blocks long.

9 Write the largest possible number using the digits 1, 4 and 6. ______

10 Write the number three hundred and twenty-seven. ______

11 3 + 7 ☐ 4 + 7 ☐ 2 + 9 ☐ 4 + 6 ☐ 5 + 7 ☐

 AUSTRALIAN SIGNPOST MATHS 2 MENTALS • ISBN 978 0 6557 0882 7

19:2

❶ Write the value of the coins above on the line below each one.

5c ______ ______ ______ ______ ______ ______

❷ Ros tossed a coin 30 times and recorded the results below.
Use these results to complete the graph.

H	T	H	T	T	H	T	H	H	T	H	H	T	H	H
H	H	H	T	H	T	H	H	T	T	H	T	T	T	T

a Complete the table to show the coins Ros tossed.

	Tally	Number
H		
T		

b Colour one box for each toss of the coin.

Heads																				
Tails																				

c Which was tossed more often, heads or tails? ______

19:3

10, 20, 30, ______, ______, ______, ______, ______

❶ **a** Count by 2s, starting at 1, then starting at 2.

1, 3, 5, ______, ______ 2, 4, 6, ______, ______

b Count forwards and backwards by 5s.

5, 10, 15, ______, ______ 50, 45, 40, ______, ______

c Count backwards by 2s.

19, 17, 15, ______, ______ 20, 18, 16, ______, ______

Learn the days of the week and the months of the year.

5, 15, 25, ____, ____, ____, ____, ____

❶

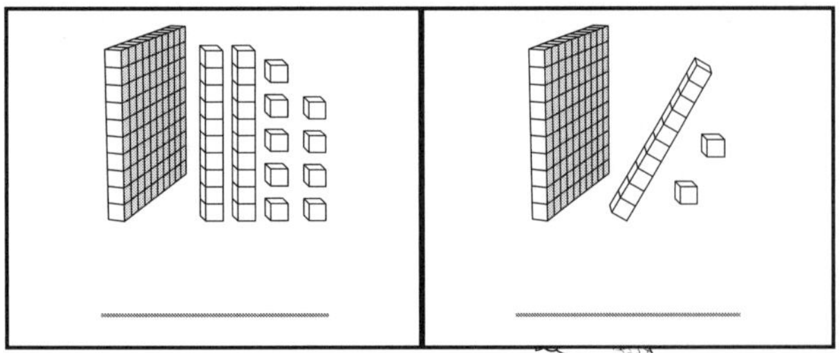

❷ Write the largest possible number using the digits 3, 5 and 9. ____

❸ Write the number four hundred and sixty-two. ____

❹

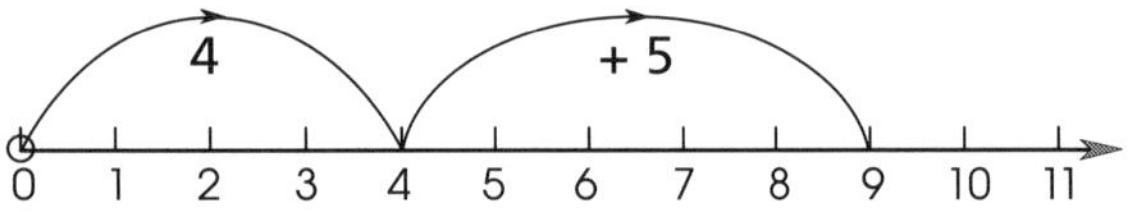

4 + 5 = ____

❺ Use 5 + 6 = 11 to find:

a 5 + 16 = ____

b 5 + 26 = ____

❻ Draw a mat with a larger area.

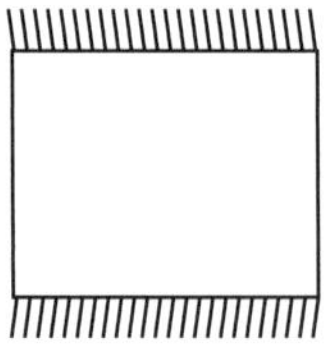

❼ Finish each number pattern.

a 12, 14, 16, ____, ____

b 5, 10, 15, ____, ____

c 7, 9, 11, ____, ____

d 30, 25, 20, ____, ____

❽ Each bundle has 10 tens. What number is modelled here? ____

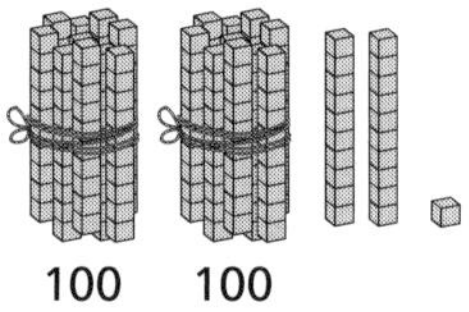

❾ Circle the largest number and write the numbers in order.

682 199 400 509

____

❿ Write the area of each shape.

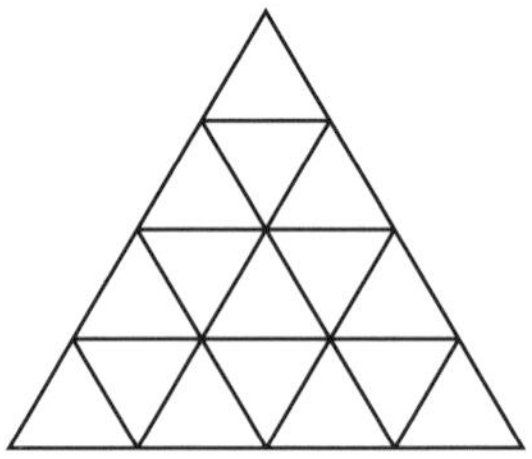

____ triangles ____ rhombuses

⓫ 7 + 5 ☐ 8 + 6 ☐ 9 + 4 ☐ 6 + 7 ☐ 7 + 6 ☐

 ISBN 978 0 6557 0882 7

20:2 13, 23, 33, ____, ____, ____, ____, ____

❶ 415 = 41 tens and 5 ones. There are 41 groups of 10 in 415.

a 538 = ____ tens ____ ones **b** 829 = ____ tens ____ ones

How many groups of 10 in: **c** 450? ____ **d** 529? ____

❷ **a** Use **9 + 5 = 14** to find: 9 + ____ = 24 and 9 + ____ = 34

b Use **6 + 5 = 11** to find: 6 + ____ = 21 and 6 + ____ = 31

❸ Write the number after:

a 119 ____ **b** 131 ____ **c** 127 ____

❹ Write the number before:

a ____ 117 **b** ____ 130 **c** ____ 103

71	72	73	74	75	76	77	78	79	80
81	82	83	84	85	86	87	88	89	90
91	92	93	94	95	96	97	98	99	100
101	102	103	104	105	106	107	108	109	110
111	112	113	114	115	116	117	118	119	120
121	122	123	124	125	126	127	128	129	130
131	132	133	134	135	136	137	138	139	140

❺ 8 + 8 ☐ 7 + 9 ☐ 9 + 9 ☐ 6 + 8 ☐ 9 + 7 ☐

20:3 18, 28, 38, ____, ____, ____, ____, ____

❶ Write a number sentence to match each number line.

a

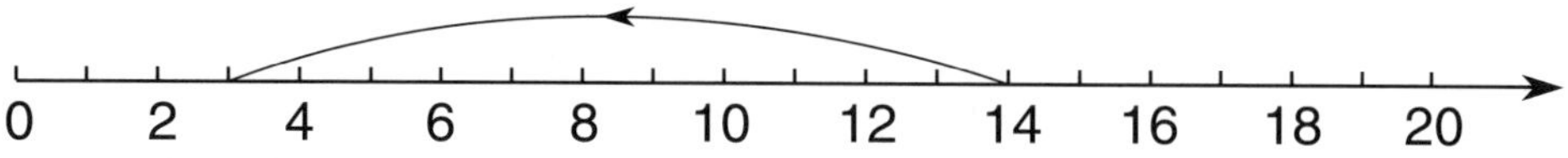

☐ − ☐ = ☐

b

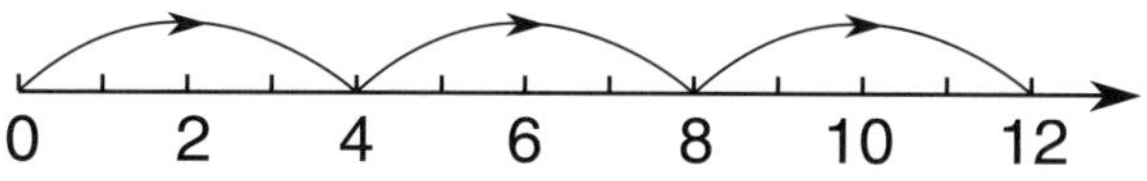

☐ groups of ☐ = ☐

❷ Make up your own number sentences. Show them on the number line.

a

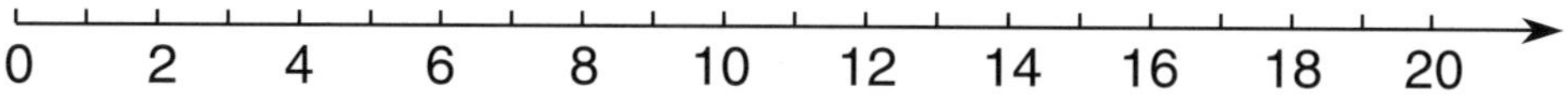

☐

b

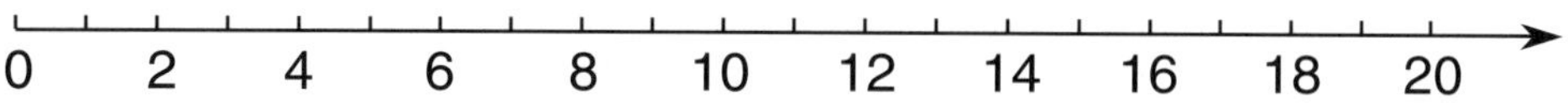

☐

☐ groups of ☐ balls = ☐

AUSTRALIAN SIGNPOST MATHS 2 MENTALS • ISBN 978 0 6557 0882 7

4, 14, 24, ______, ______, ______, ______, ______

1

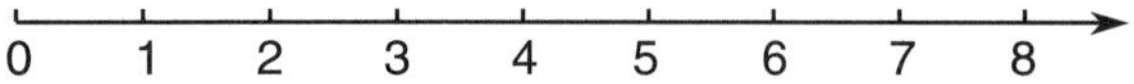

5 + 3 = ______ 3 + 5 = ______

8 – 3 = ______ 8 – 5 = ______

2 Draw lines to match.

5c 10c 20c 50c

3 Circle the shape with the smallest area.

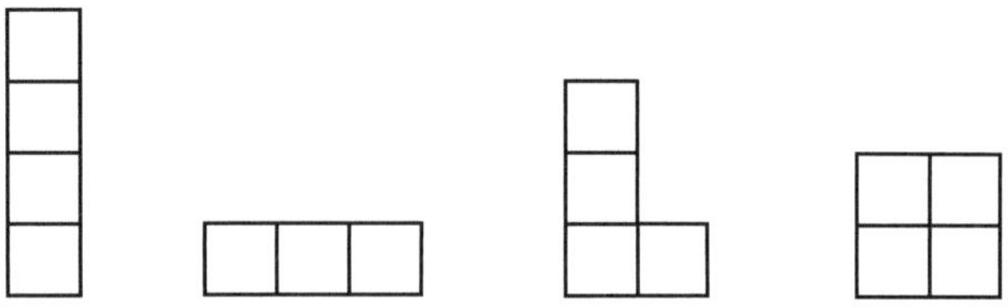

4 Use 5 + 7 = 12 to find:

a 5 + 17 = ______

b 5 + 27 = ______

5

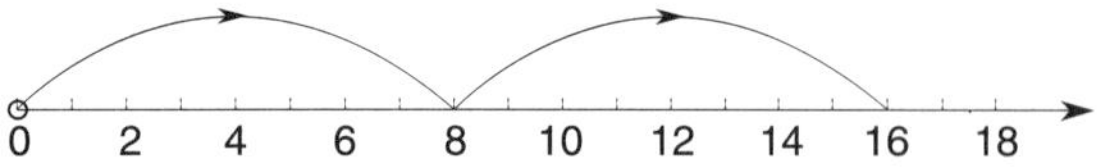

Complete:

______ + ______ = ______

6

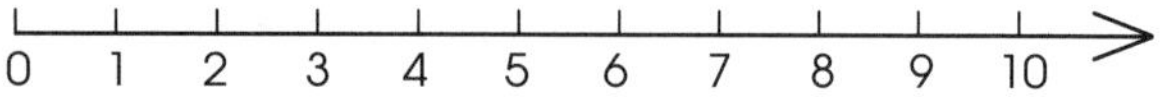

This is called a

n ______________ l ______________.

7 What is the area of this shape?

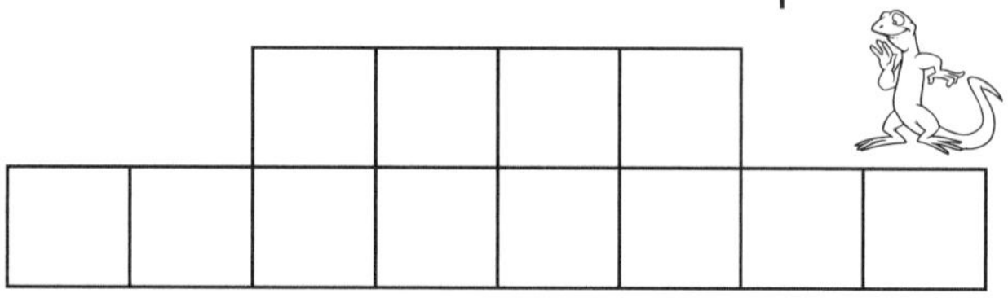

Area = _____ squares

8 Draw a shape with an area of 10 squares on this grid.

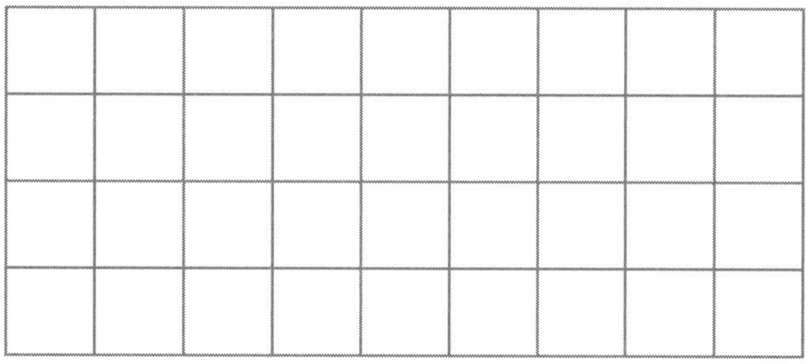

9 Draw each line of symmetry.

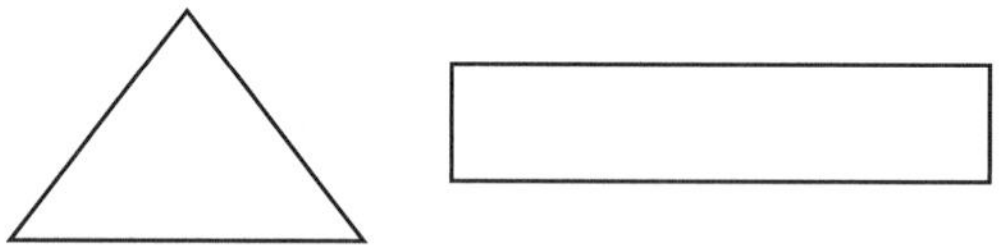

10 Circle the shapes where a line of symmetry is shown correctly.

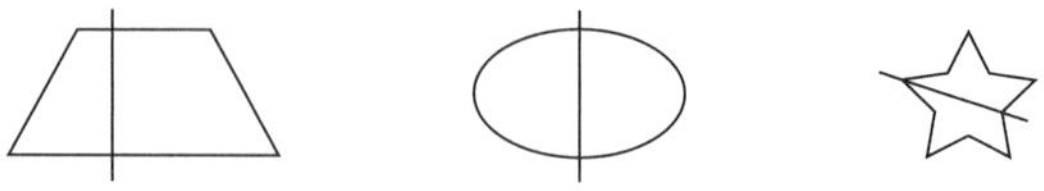

11 2 + 7 ☐ 4 + 5 ☐ 2 + 8 ☐ 5 + 6 ☐ 3 + 8 ☐

21:2

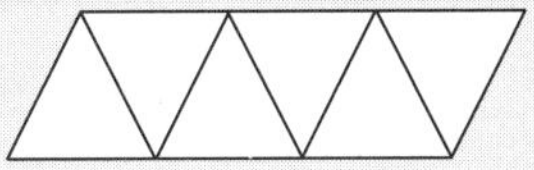

Area = ____ triangles

❶ Match each coin to its name.

one dollar   fifty cents   twenty cents   two dollars

❷ Match each note with its name.

$5.00	$10.00	$20.00	$50.00	$100.00

❸

6	5	3	7	4
+ 2	+ 2	+ 2	+ 2	+ 2
____	____	____	____	____

21:3

30, 35, 40, 45, 50, 55, 60, ____, ____, ____

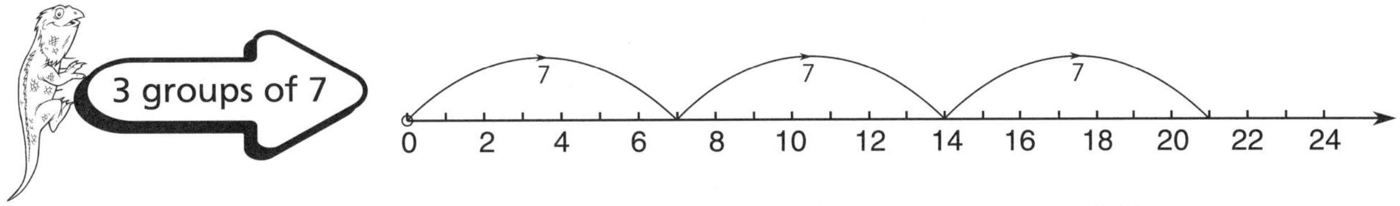

❶ **a** 8 + 4 + 5 ____

b 3 groups of 7 ____

c 24 – 5 – 7 ____

d 10 + 3 + 8 ____

e 2 groups of 7 ____

f 2 groups of 8 ____

g 3 + 8 + 5 + 7 ____

h 4 groups of 6 ____

Total =

❶ How many groups of 100 are in:

a 341? ____ b 730? ____

❷ How many 10-cent coins in:

a $1.20? ____ b $3? ____

❸ 653 = 65 tens and 3 ones

534 = ____ tens ____ ones

❹ How many groups of 10 are in:

a 410? ____ b 527? ____

❺

____ rows of ____ = ____

❻ Draw a shape with an area of 12 square units on this grid.

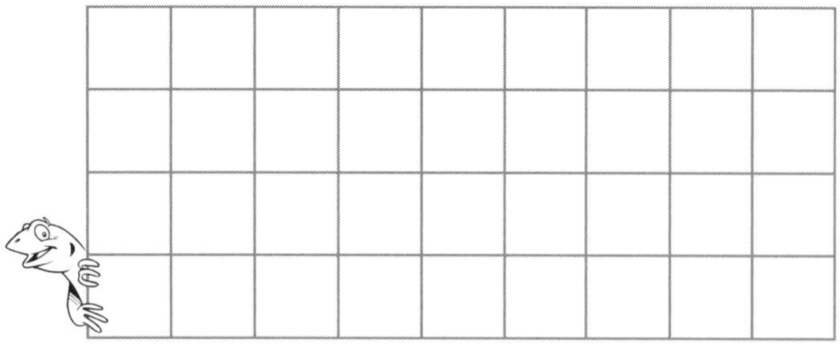

❼ Draw each line of symmetry.

❽ What is the total value? ____

❾ Write the value of each note.

____ ____

❿ Colour the larger number in each pair.

127	179	100	172
170	180	189	170

⓫ Write the number after:

a 421 ____ b 893 ____

⓬ How much altogether?

____ c

⓭ 4 + 9 ☐ 5 + 8 ☐ 8 + 7 ☐ 7 + 8 ☐ 8 + 9 ☐

 ISBN 978 0 6557 0882 7

22:2

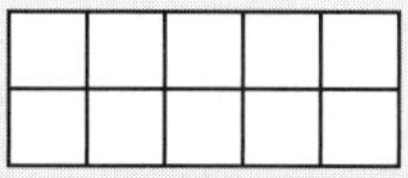

Area = ____ squares

❶ Circle the coins with a value of less than 20 cents.
Colour the silver coins grey and the gold coins yellow.

How much money altogether? ______

❷ Write the area of each shape. Colour the shape or shapes with the largest area.

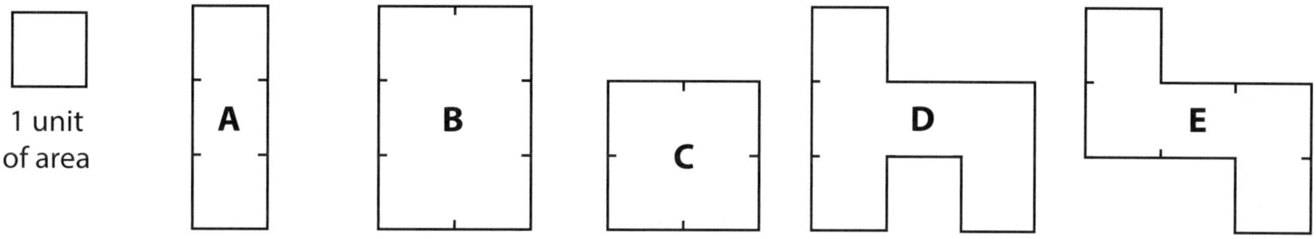

______ units   ______ units   ______ units   ______ units   ______ units

❸ 638 = 63 tens and 8 ones. There are 63 groups of 10 in 638.

a 392 = ______ tens ______ ones   **b** 543 = ______ tens ______ ones

How many groups of 10 in: **c** 380? ______ **d** 727? ______

22:3

❶ Draw three coins in each money box to make:

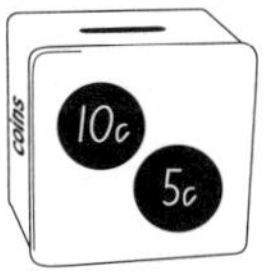

= fifteen cents

a forty-five cents

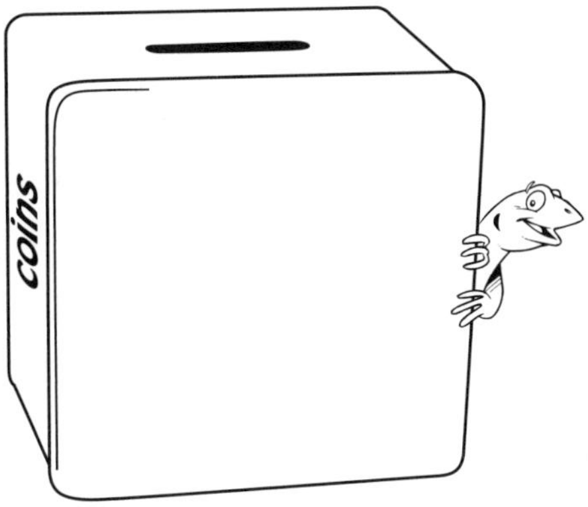

b sixty cents

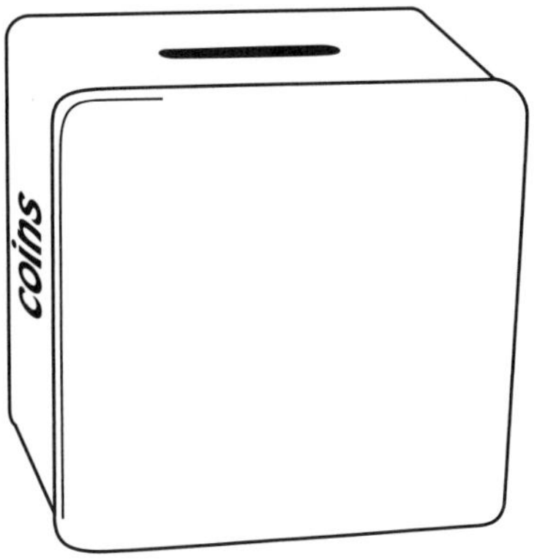

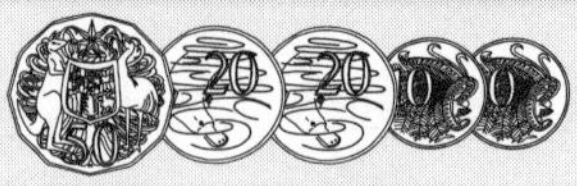

1 How many groups of 100 are in:

a 521? ______ **b** 869? ______

2 How many 10-cent coins in:

a $1? ______ **b** $5? ______

3 825 = 82 tens and 5 ones

257 = ______ tens ______ ones

4 How many groups of 10 are in:

a 162? ______ **b** 423? ______

c 837? ______ **d** 108? ______

5 Circle words that describe this object.

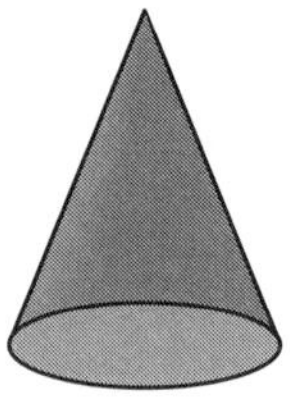

cone	prism
curved	flat
rolls	slides

6 Circle groups of five.

How many groups of 5? ______

How many altogether? ______

7 567 = ________ tens ________ ones

8 How much money is shown here?

______

9 Show how you could make 20 cents using 4 coins.

10 Circle the objects that have curved surfaces.

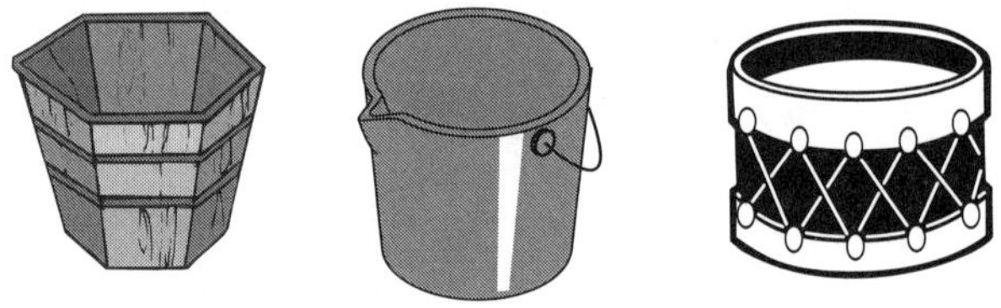

11 Complete the cylinder.

How many:

surfaces? ______

flat surfaces? ______

curved surfaces? ______

12

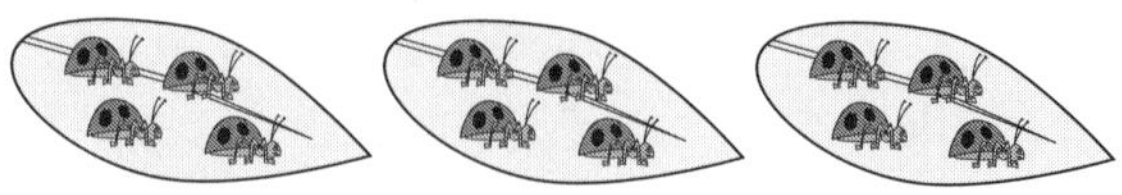

a How many bugs? ______

b How many groups? ______

c How many bugs in each group? ______

13 4 + 3 ☐ 6 + 4 ☐ 9 + 10 ☐ 3 + 3 ☐ 7 + 2 ☐

23:2

Total = ☐

❶ Circle the coins that make 60c.

❷ Look at the pictures on the right.

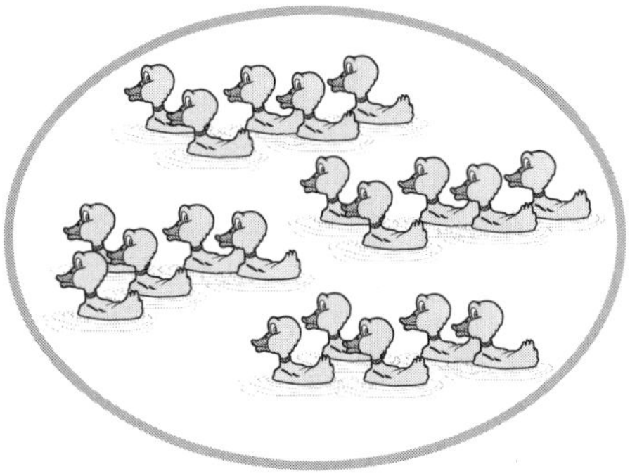

a How many ducks? ____

b How many groups? ____

c How many ducks in each group? ____

❸ Colour one flat surface on each 3D object.

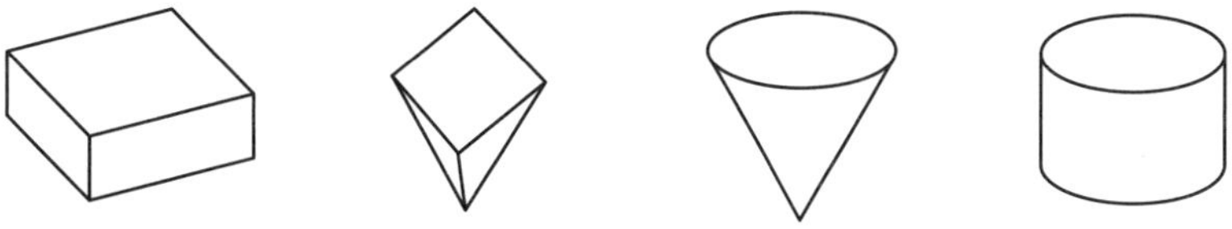

❹ 10 + 6 ☐ 10 + 9 ☐ 10 + 7 ☐ 10 + 8 ☐ 10 + 10 ☐

23:3

3 groups of ☐ **=** ☐

❶ Write the total for each set of coins.

a

____

b

____

c

____

d

____

3 groups of ☐ = ☐

❶ Build to the next 10 to find:

a 19 + 4 = 19 + 1 + _____ = _____

b 18 + 3 = 18 + 2 + _____ = _____

c 19 + 5 = _____

❷ Draw a square at each right angle in these shapes. Draw a dot in all the angles that are greater than a right angle.

❸

What is the total value? __________

❹ Rows of 4 cylinders:

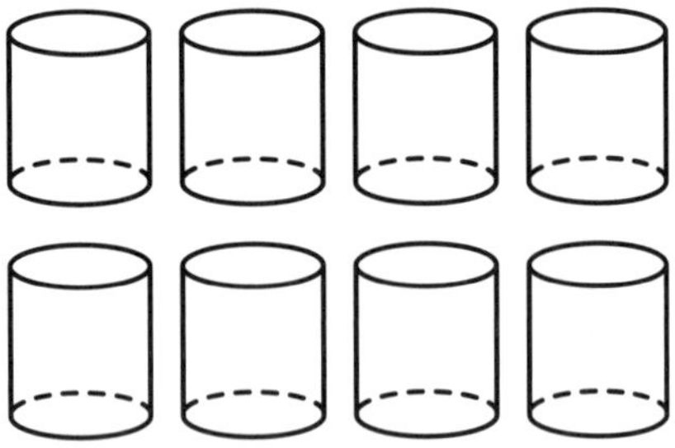

a How many cylinders? _____

b How many rows? _____

c How many cylinders in each row? _____

❺ Complete the cone.

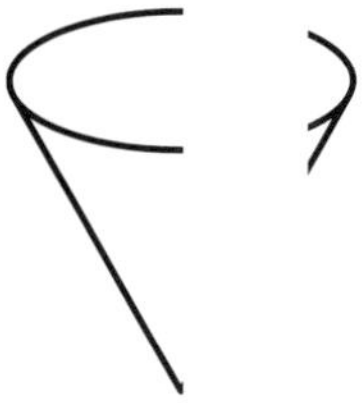

How many:

surfaces? _____

flat surfaces? _____

curved surfaces? _____

❻ What number does this tally show?

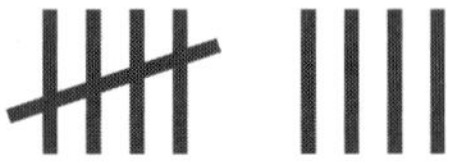

_____

❼ Draw dots, then complete each number sentence.

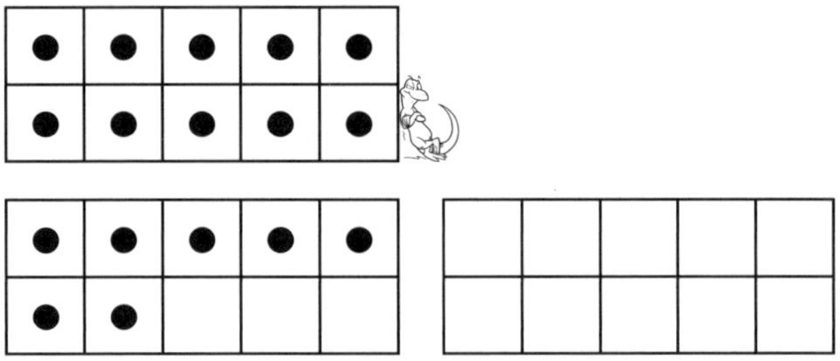

17 + 6 = 17 + _____ + _____

= _____ + _____

= _____

❽ Show how you could make 60 cents using 4 coins.

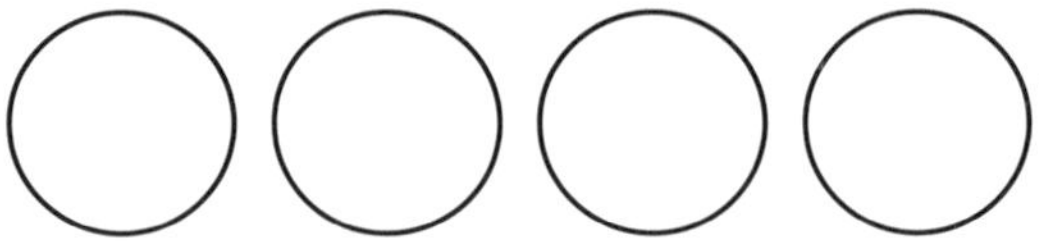

❾ This is a c __________.

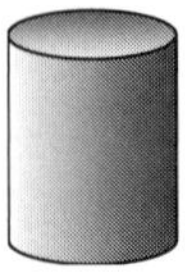

Its ends are circles and it has one curved surface.

 AUSTRALIAN SIGNPOST MATHS 2 MENTALS • ISBN 978 0 6557 0882 7

24:2

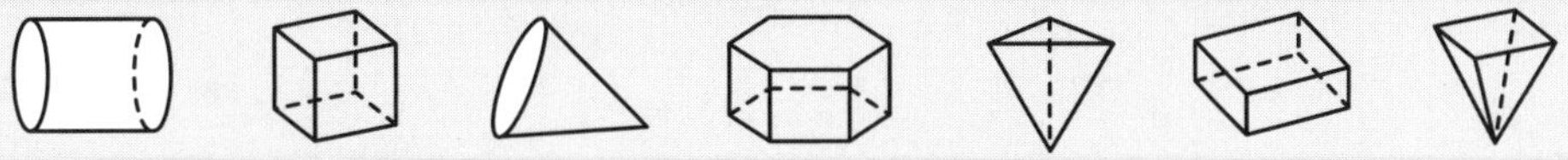

❶ Colour one flat surface on each object above.

❷ Circle the coins that will add to give the value of the first coin.

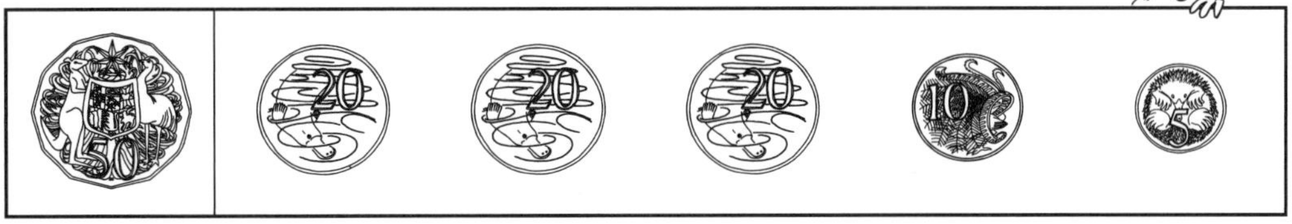

❸

+	7	5	8	6	9	4
3						
5						

	10	7	9	5	8	6
− 5						
− 3						

❹ Copy each object and draw a line to match it with its name.

cone cylinder cube prism

 ☐ 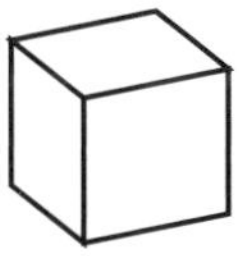 ☐  ☐ 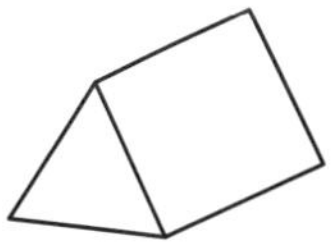 ☐

❺ 9 + 8 ☐ 8 + 5 ☐ 7 + 10 ☐ 9 + 10 ☐ 6 + 10 ☐

24:3

10c 20c ☐ , 5c 20c ☐ , 10c 10c 10c ☐

❶ How much money?

a  ______

b  ______

c  ______

d  ______

e  ______

f  ______

How many? ☐

25:1

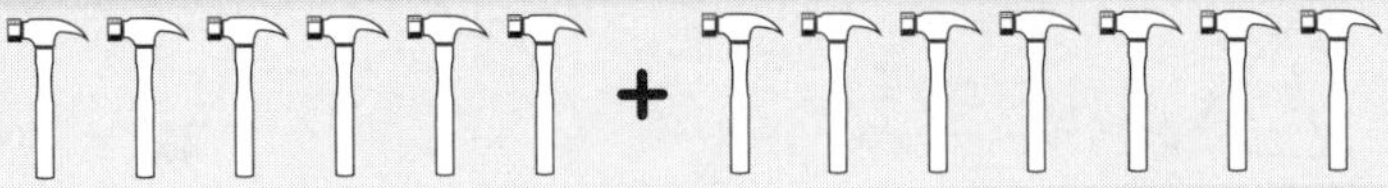 , ☐ + ☐ = ☐

1 Make each sum add to 10.

9 + ______ 7 + ______

8 + ______ 6 + ______

2 Draw dots, then complete each number sentence.

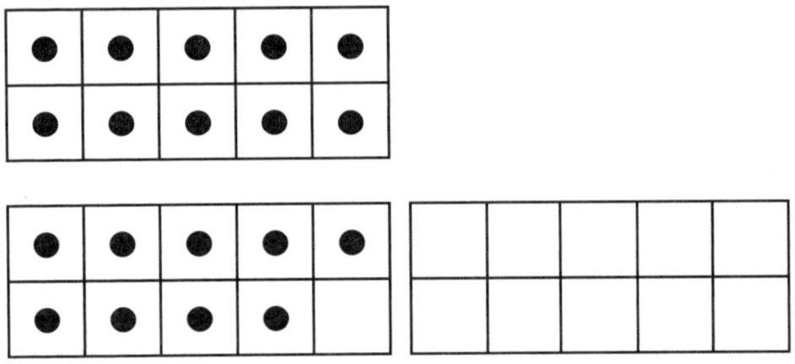

19 + 7 = 19 + ______ + ______

= 20 + ______

= ______

3 Build to the next 10 to find:

28 + 5 = ______ 37 + 6 = ______

48 + 7 = ______ 56 + 7 = ______

4 Draw a square at each right angle in these shapes. Draw a dot in all the angles that are greater than a right angle.

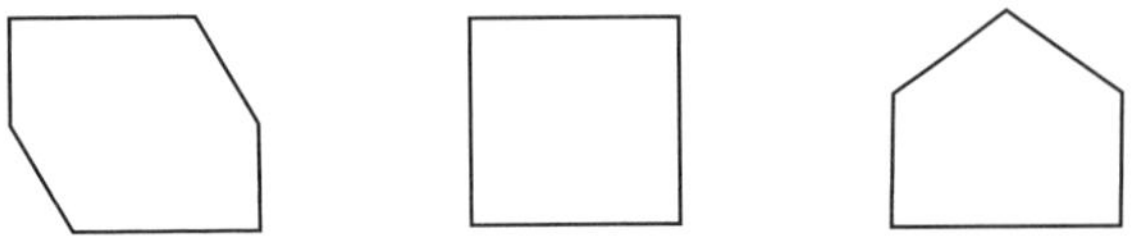

5 This is a tally. What number does it represent? ______

6 Circle the lighter side.

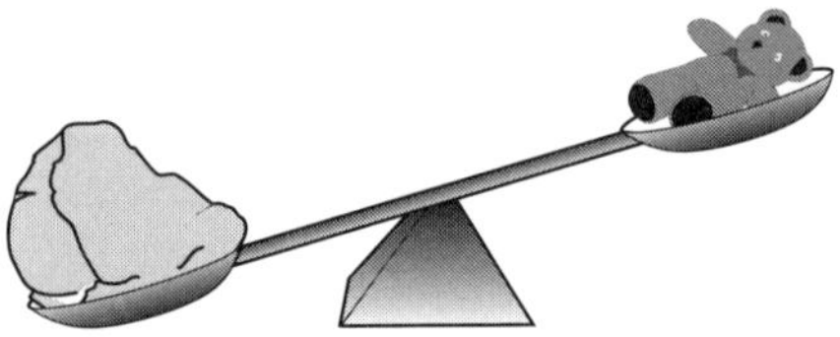

7 70 + 20 = ______ 50 + 30 = ______

4 + 5 = ______ 7 + 2 = ______

8 Use the split strategy to find:

35 + 52 = ______ 41 + 54 = ______

21 + 17 = ______ 26 + 12 = ______

9 Use this list to complete the graph and table.

List: yes, no, no, yes, no, no

Table

yes	
no	

Graph

yes	no

10 4 + 5 ☐ 5 + 4 ☐ 3 + 6 ☐ 6 + 3 ☐ 6 + 4 ☐

 ISBN 978 0 6557 0882 7

25:2 21, 31, 41, ____, ____, ____, ____, ____

❶ Write the numeral and words for each number shown.

a | 4 | hundreds | 3 | tens | 2 | ones | ☐ ____________________

b | 2 | hundreds | 9 | tens | 4 | ones | ☐ ____________________

c | 7 | hundreds | 0 | tens | 5 | ones | ☐ ____________________

❷ 3 + 9 ☐ 4 + 8 ☐ 6 + 9 ☐ 5 + 9 ☐ 6 + 8 ☐

25:3 145, 146, 147, ____, ____, ____, ____, ____

❶ Complete each number bond house.
Each row adds to make the number at the top of the house.

7	
1	
	4
6	
5	
2	
4	

8	
	7
4	
	1
2	
	3
6	
	5

9	
	8
6	
2	
	5
	1
3	
7	
	4

10	
	9
6	
	7
4	
	5
2	
	3
8	
1	

26:1

❶ Build to the next 10 to find:

47 + 7 = ____ 69 + 4 = ____

258 + 6 = ____ 138 + 5 = ____

347 + 5 = ____ 429 + 3 = ____

❷ Use the split strategy to find:

63 + 22 = ____ 84 + 13 = ____

25 + 14 = ____ 74 + 25 = ____

36 + 41 = ____ 62 + 36 = ____

❸ How many more do you need to get to 50?

a 42 ____ **b** 46 ____

c 41 ____ **d** 44 ____

❹ How many more do you need to get to 470?

a 465 ____ **b** 468 ____

c 462 ____ **d** 463 ____

❺ How many 10c coins in:

a $2? ____ **b** $2.10? ____

c $3.40? ____ **d** $3.55? ____

e $9.70? ____ **f** $8.45? ____

❻ 40 + 10 = ____ 30 + 20 = ____

60 + 30 = ____ 50 + 40 = ____

❼ Has the fish a greater or smaller mass than the pencil? ____________

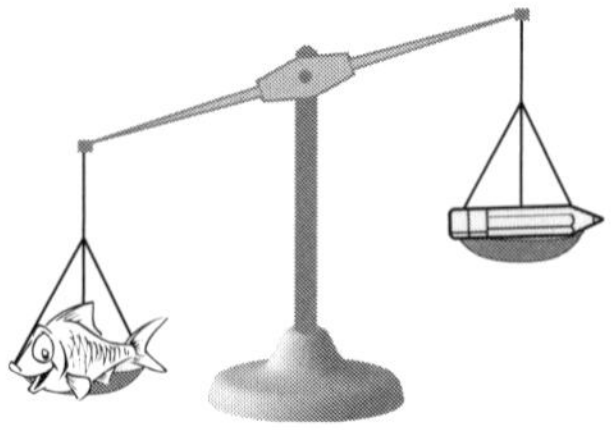

❽ 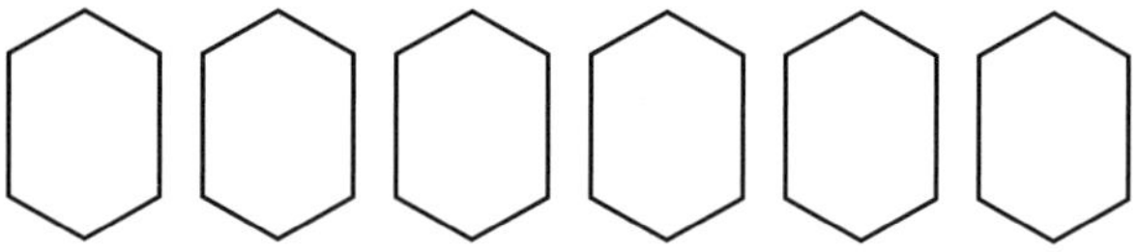

6 hexagons. How many groups of 2 can be circled? ____

6 – 2 – 2 – 2 = ____

❾ The first triangle is turned a quarter turn to the right. Colour the shape it becomes.

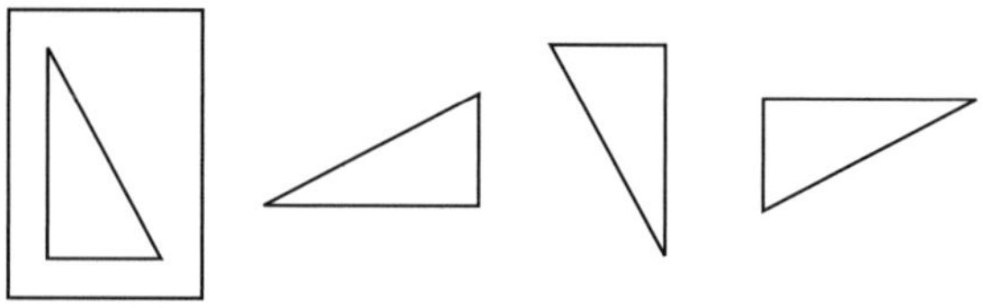

❿ Draw something else that would balance the orange.

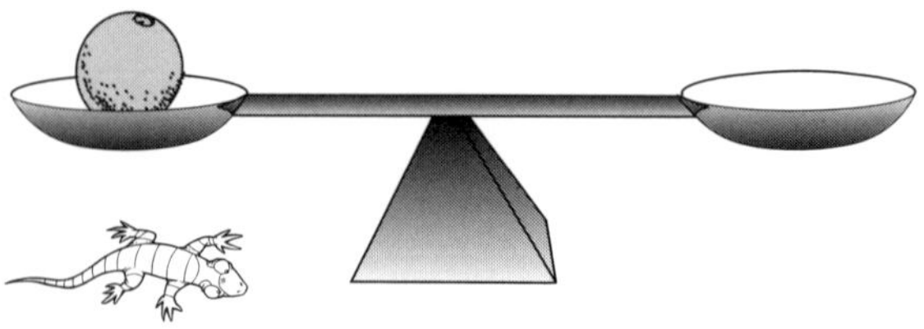

26:2 145, 146, 147, ____, ____, ____, ____, ____, ____

❶ **a** 8 – 2 – 2 – 2 = ____ **b** 10 – 2 – 2 – 2 = ____

❷ Circle the one with the smaller mass.

 or 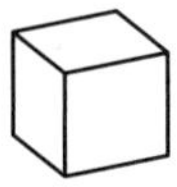

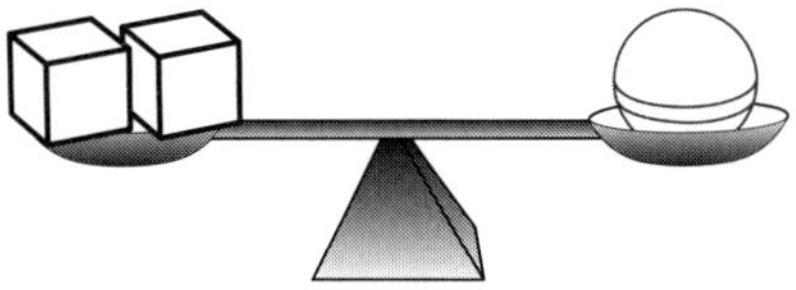

❸ Use the split strategy to answer these sums.

32 + 43 = ________ 61 + 24 = ________ 72 + 25 = ________

❹ **a** 14 pencils. 5 broken.

How many are left? ______

b 17 books. 9 borrowed.

How many are left? ______

❺ 362 = ____ hundreds ____ tens ____ ones

❻ 3 + 7 ☐ 8 + 2 ☐ 4 + 6 ☐ 5 + 5 ☐ 9 + 1 ☐

26:3 134, 133, 132, ____, ____, ____, ____, ____, ____

❶ The pattern continues on the 4th picture.

a Find how the tiles change. Shade the grey tiles in the 4th picture.

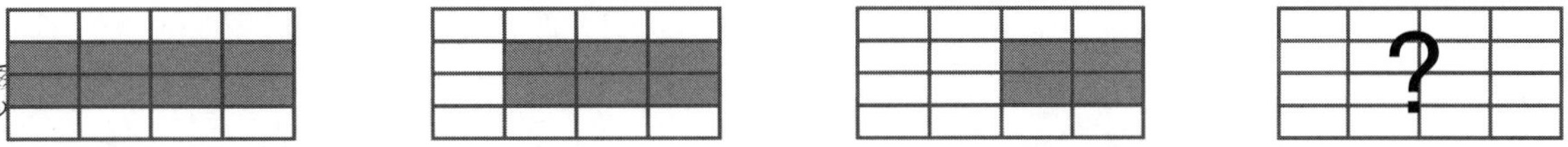

8 grey tiles	___ grey tiles	___ grey tiles	___ grey tiles
8 white tiles	___ white tiles	___ white tiles	___ white tiles

b How many grey tiles would be used altogether? ______

c How many white tiles would be used altogether? ______

How many elephants? ☐

27:1

 , 12 ÷ 2 = ☐

1 Build to the next 10 to find:

59 + 4 = _____ 87 + 6 = _____

356 + 8 = _____ 847 + 7 = _____

2 12 boats are shared by 4 people.

12 ÷ 4 = _____ Each has _____.

3 Circle the picture that is showing a turn.

4 Start at 12. Draw another hand on the clock that is a quarter turn to the right.

5 How many more do you need to get to 60?

a 53 _____ **b** 55 _____

c 57 _____ **d** 52 _____

6 How many more do you need to get to 360?

a 359 _____ **b** 358 _____

c 351 _____ **d** 354 _____

7 Use the split strategy to find:

66 + 21 = _____ 83 + 15 = _____

58 + 31 = _____ 64 + 21 = _____

8

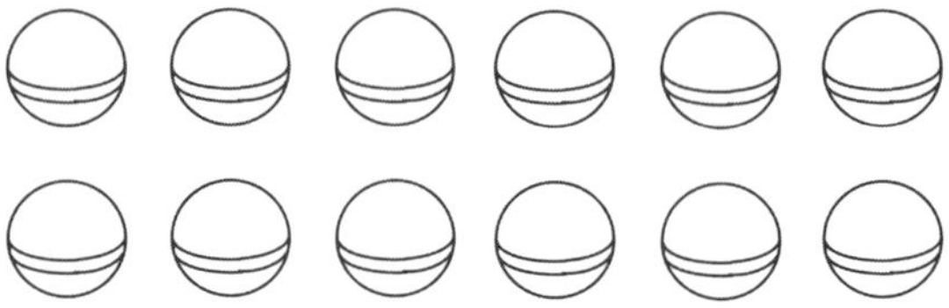

There are 12 balls.
How many children could have:

a 2 balls? _____ 12 ÷ 2 = _____

b 3 balls? _____ 12 ÷ 3 = _____

c 6 balls? _____ 12 ÷ 6 = _____

9 12 – 2 – 2 – 2 – 2 = _____

12 – 3 – 3 – 3 = _____

10 Use this list to complete the graph and table.

List

1, 4, 4, 3, 1, 4, 2, 2, 2, 4, 3

Graph

1	2	3	4

Table

1	
2	
3	
4	

 ISBN 978 0 6557 0882 7

27:2

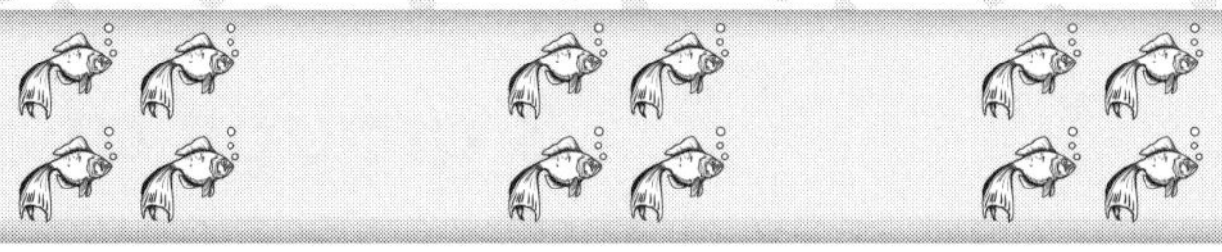

3 groups of ☐ = ☐

❶ 

- **a** How many groups of 6 apples? _____ 12 ÷ 6 = _____
- **b** How many groups of 2 apples? _____ 12 ÷ 2 = _____
- **c** How many groups of 4 apples? _____ 12 ÷ 4 = _____
- **d** How many groups of 3 apples? _____ 12 ÷ 3 = _____
- **e** How many groups of 12 apples? _____ 12 ÷ 12 = _____

❷ Complete each table.
Each stroke stands for one. A gate stands for five.

a

Object	Tally	Number
pens	||||	4
pots	卌 卌 ||	
cups	卌 |||	

b

Object	Tally	Number
hats	卌 卌 ||	
dogs	卌 卌 卌	
hens	卌 卌 卌 |	

❸ 6 + 6 ☐ 4 + 4 ☐ 2 + 2 ☐ 5 + 5 ☐ 3 + 3 ☐

27:3

2 groups of 8 = ☐

❶ Complete each number bond house.
Each row adds to make the number at the top of the house.

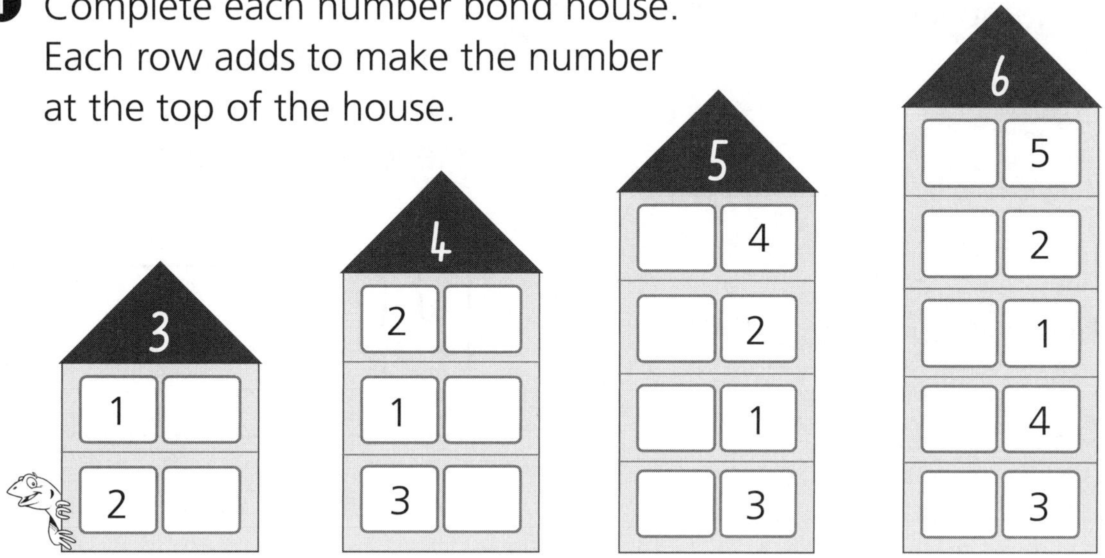

3 groups of 3 = ☐

1 Build to the next 10 to find:

28 + 4 = _____ 39 + 7 = _____

47 + 6 = _____ 38 + 5 = _____

2 Use the split strategy to find:

35 + 21 = _____

63 + 11 = _____

3 8 cars were shared by 2 children.

8 ÷ 2 = _____ Each has _____.

4 What number is shown here?

____

5 Use the jump strategy to find:

87 + 5 = _____

87

6 Use the jump strategy to find:

93 – 5 = _____

93

7 Share 10 stars among 5.

10 ÷ 5 = _____

Each has _____.

8

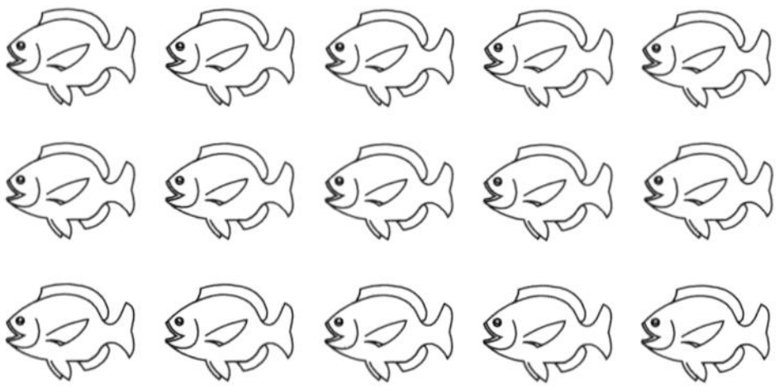

a How many fish? _____

How many:

b groups of 3? _____

15 ÷ 3 = _____

c groups of 5? _____

15 ÷ 5 = _____

9 Write the number before:

a 538 ______ **b** 461 ______

10 Use tally marks to record how many times you can see the letters **d** and **f** on this page.

d	
f	

Which letter was used more? _____

 • *AUSTRALIAN SIGNPOST MATHS 2 MENTALS* • ISBN 978 0 6557 0882 7

28:2  4 groups of ☐ = ☐

❶ Use the jump strategy to find:

a 49 + 4 = _____

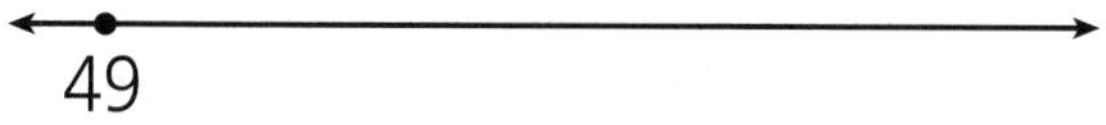

b 78 + 15 = _____

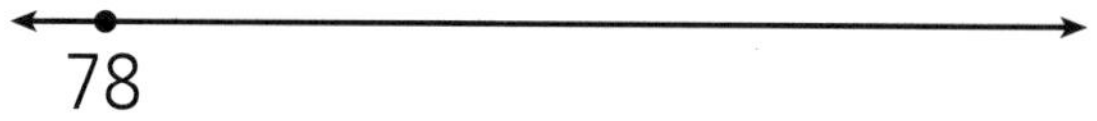

c 54 – 6 = _____

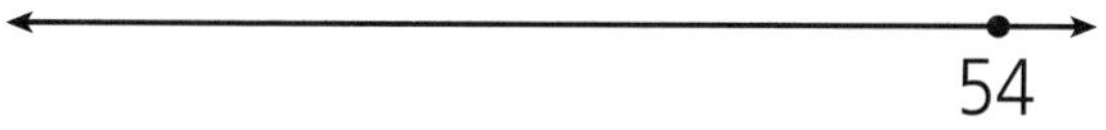

d 81 – 17 = _____

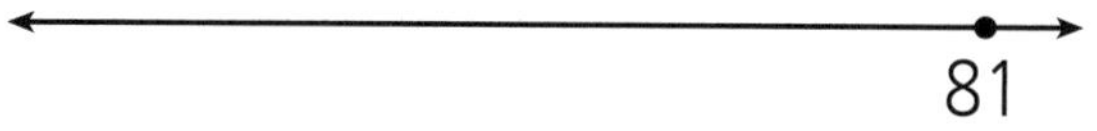

❷ I am standing at X. Where would I be if I move:

a 1 left then 4 forward? _____

b 3 forward then 1 left? _____

c 5 forward, 2 right then 5 down? _____

front

D		G		
	F		H	
	C			
			E	
A				
		X		B

↑

❸ 576 = _____ hundreds _____ tens _____ ones

❹ 10 + 4 ☐ 10 + 7 ☐ 10 + 3 ☐ 10 + 9 ☐ 10 + 6 ☐

28:3 To add 9, you can add 10 first then take away _____.

❶ Complete each number web.

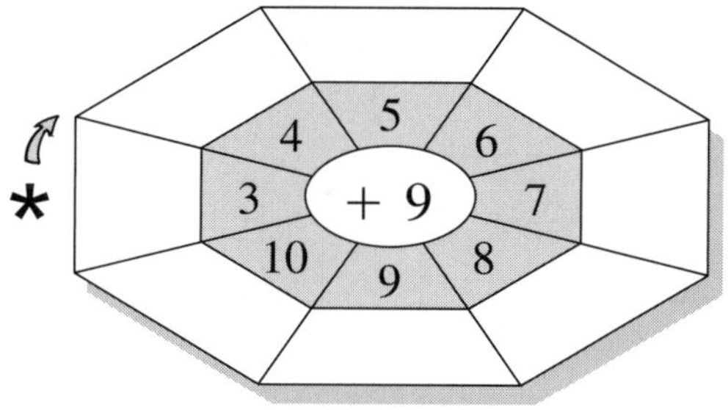

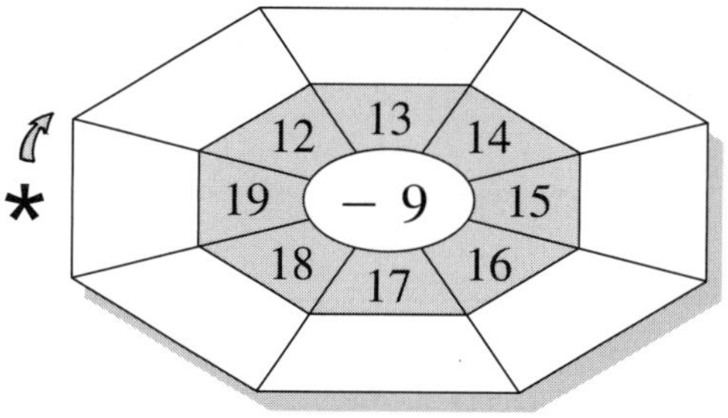

127, 128, _____, _____, 131, _____, 133

1. Use the jump strategy to find:

   48 + 32 = _____

48

2. Use the jump strategy to find:

   74 – 38 = _____

74

3. What number is shown here?

_____

4. Circle one quarter of this group.

5. a Draw a line to cut this rectangle into halves. Colour one half.

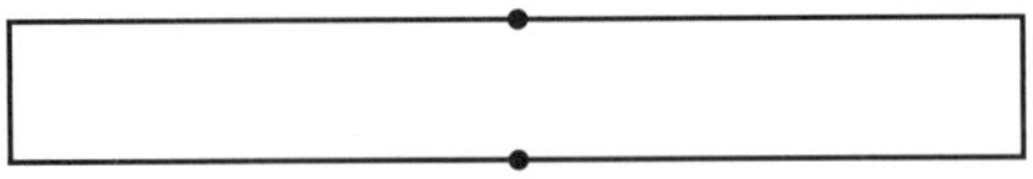

   b Draw lines to cut this rectangle into quarters. Colour one quarter.

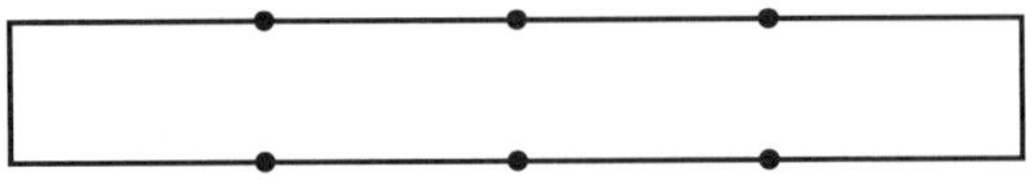

6. Share 12 cans among 4.

   12 ÷ 4 = _____

   Each has _____ cans.

7. 328 = 32 tens and 8 ones

   a 436 = _____ tens _____ ones

   b 386 = _____ tens _____ ones

8. How many groups of 10 are in:

   a 140? _____ b 241? _____

9. 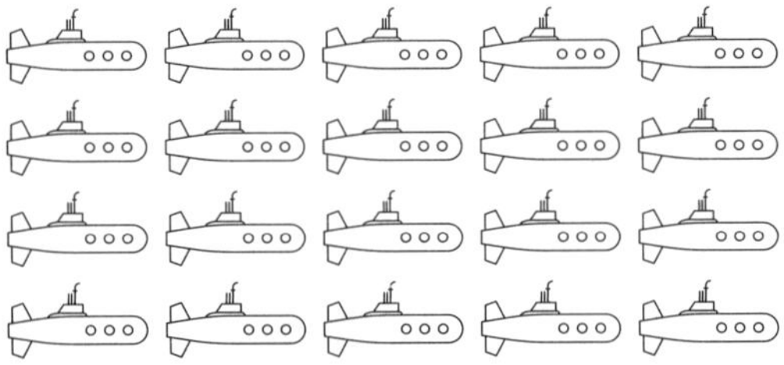

   20 submarines. How many:

   a groups of 2? _____

   20 ÷ 2 = _____

   b groups of 4? _____

   20 ÷ 4 = _____

   c groups of 5? _____

   20 ÷ 5 = _____

10. What number is shown here?

_____

 • *AUSTRALIAN SIGNPOST MATHS 2 MENTALS* • ISBN 978 0 6557 0882 7

29:2

☐ eagles

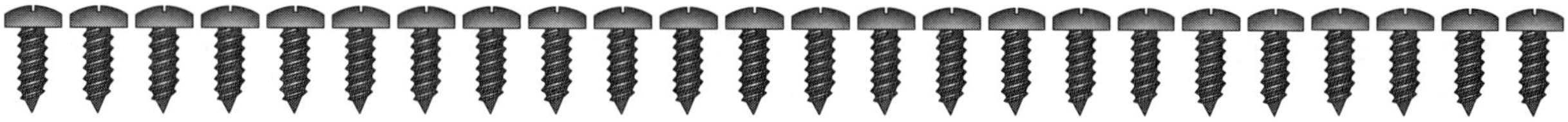

❶ How many groups of: 6 nails? _____ 4 nails? _____ 3 nails? _____

❷ Four boys shared these masks. One fair share was _____.

❸ Adam started at **A**. He moved two rectangles to the right, 3 rectangles down and 1 rectangle to the left.

Write a **B** in the rectangle where he finished.

A			

❹ Circle the pictures that show halves. Tick the picture that shows quarters.

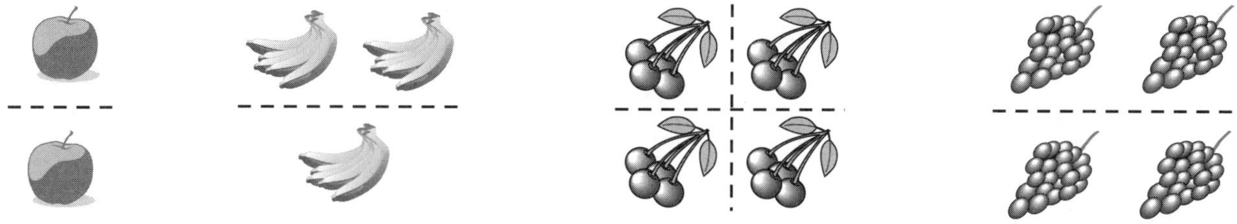

❺ 9 + 9 ☐ 8 + 8 ☐ 7 + 7 ☐ 6 + 6 ☐ 5 + 5 ☐

29:3

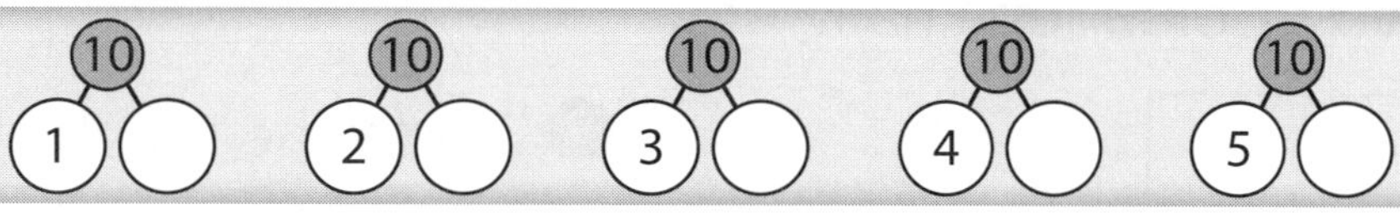

❶ **Jo's timetable**

1 o'clock	pool
2 o'clock	shops
3 o'clock	park
4 o'clock	home
5 o'clock	beach

Where was Jo:

a at 3 o'clock? __________

b at 5 o'clock? __________

c 2 hours after she was at the shops? __________

d 3 hours before she was at home? __________

e 4 hours after she was at the pool? __________

30:1 January, February, Autumn: March, April, May, Winter: June, July, August, Spring: September, October, November, Summer: December

❶ Use the jump strategy to find:

26 + 47 = _____

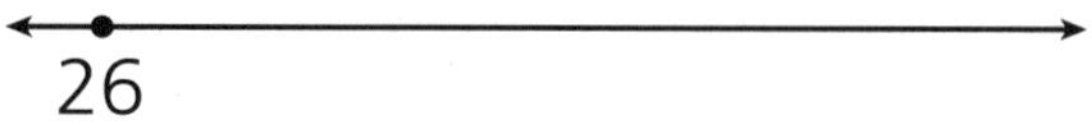

❷ Use the jump strategy to find:

83 – 26 = ___________

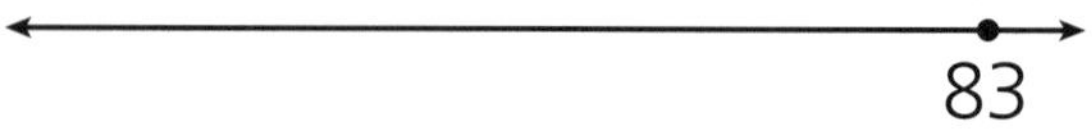

❸

______ groups of ______ = ______

2 + 2 + 2 + 2 + 2 = ______

5 × 2 = ______

❹ **a** Draw a line to cut this rectangle into halves. Colour one half.

b Draw lines to cut this rectangle into quarters. Colour one quarter.

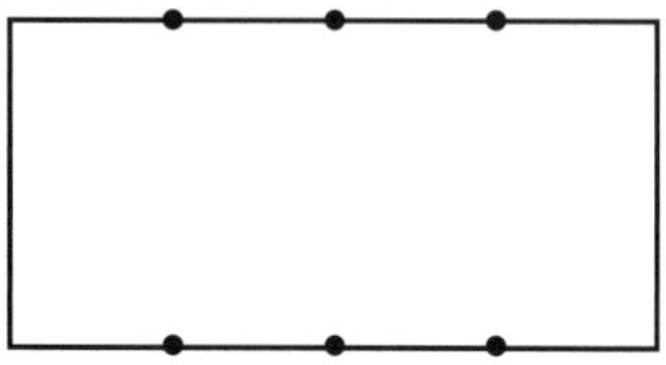

❺ How many months in 1 year?

____

❻ Write the months in spring.

____

____

____

❼ Write the months in winter.

____

____

____

❽ How many months is it from the beginning of summer to the end of autumn?

_____ months

❾ Write the number after:

a 217 ______ **b** 138 ______

c 536 ______ **d** 391 ______

❿ Circle half of the cupcakes.
Colour one quarter of the cupcakes.

30:2 , ☐ groups of ☐ = ☐

1. Circle the groups that are divided into quarters.

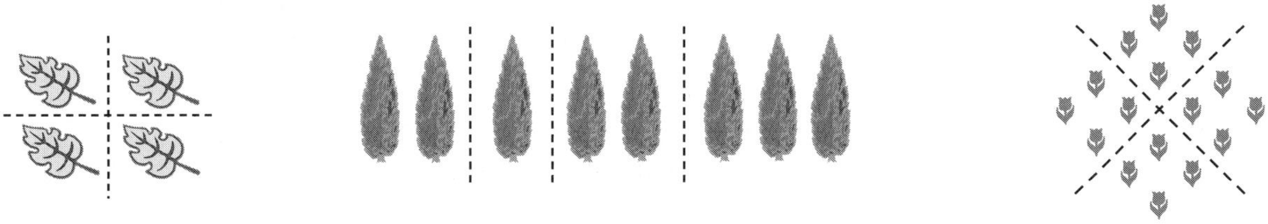

2. a Draw a line to mark the halfway point of these footballs.
   b How many in each half? _____
   c How many altogether? _____
   d Draw a line to mark the halfway point of each half.
   e How many in each quarter? _____

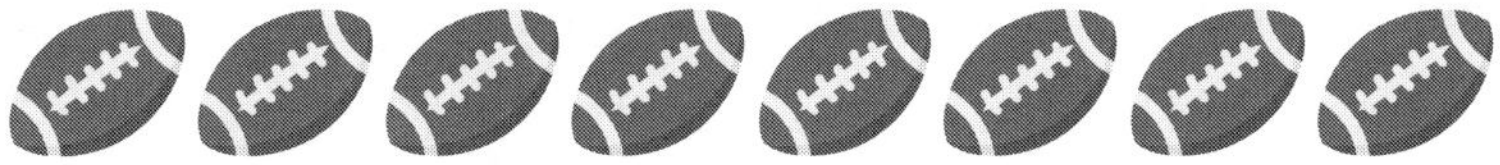

3. Use the split strategy to answer these sums:

   a 31 + 22 = ______   b 71 + 24 = ______   c 15 + 42 = ______

4. a 32 + 19 = ______   b 64 – 26 = ______

30:3  ☐,  ☐,  ☐

1. We graphed the weather for one month.

A

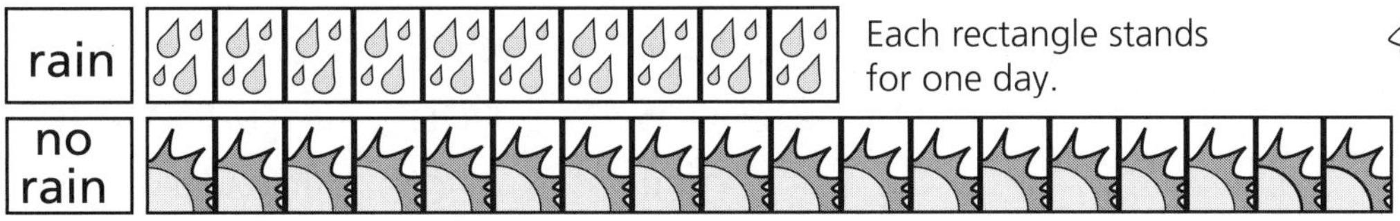

Each rectangle stands for one day.

   a Circle the correct answer.

   Graph **A** above is a dot / picture / column / pie graph.

   Graph **B**, on the right, is a picture / column / pie graph.

   b Do these two graphs show the same data? _____

   c Which graph is easier to understand, **A** or **B**? _____

B

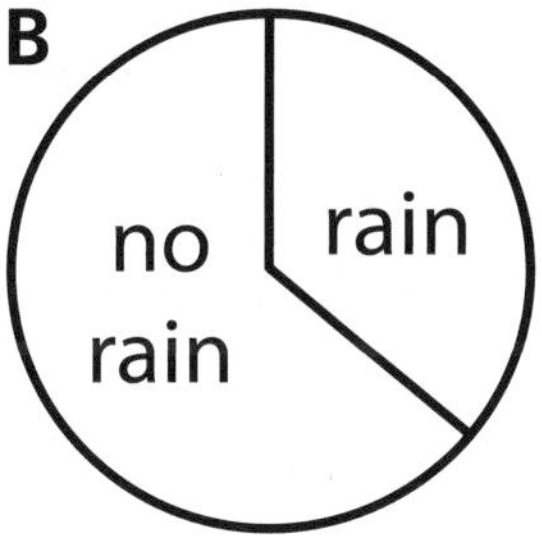

 • *AUSTRALIAN SIGNPOST MATHS 2 MENTALS* • ISBN 978 0 6557 0882 7

❶ 8 + 6 = ____ 7 + 9 = ____ 6 + 8 = ____ 8 + 7 = ____

❷ The number after 365 is ________ .

❸ a Draw a line to cut this group in half.

b How many in each half? _____

c Draw more lines to halve each half.

d How many in each quarter? _________

❹ A can holds 3 balls.

How many balls in:

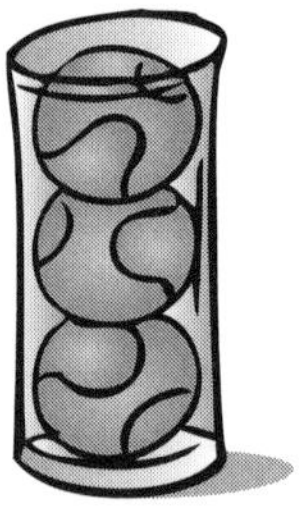

a 3 cans? _____

b 5 cans? _____

c 7 cans? _____

❺ How many of these cans can we fill with 15 balls? _____

❻ Draw a shape that has parallel lines.

❼ Trace the shapes above. Say out loud the name and the number of sides and vertices for each shape.

❽ Use arrows to show which are parallel on the shapes above.

❾ How many months are in one year? ___________

❿ Circle:
One **half / quarter** is shaded.

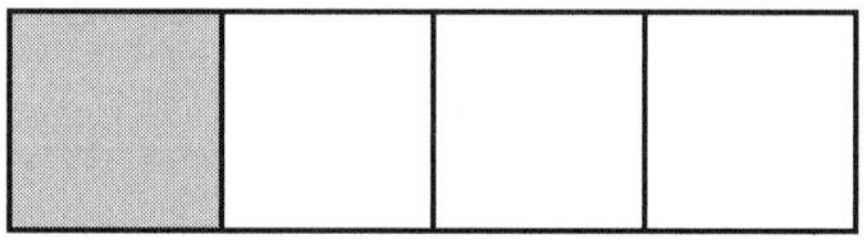

⓫ 10 – 2 – 2 – 2 – 2 = _____

⓬

A			

Lydia started at **A**. She went 2 down, 3 right, 1 up and 2 left. Colour the rectangle where she finished.

⓭ 6 + 5 ☐ 6 + 7 ☐ 9 + 8 ☐ 7 + 8 ☐ 7 + 6 ☐

 ISBN 978 0 6557 0882 7

31:2 3, 6, 9, ____, ____, ____, ____, ____, ____

❶ a Draw a line to mark the halfway point of these ovals.

b How many in each half? ____

c How many altogether? ____

d Draw a line to mark the halfway point of each half.

e How many in each quarter? ____

❷

July						
S	M	T	W	T	F	S
				1	2	3
4	5	6	7	8	9	10
11	12	13	14	15	16	17
18	19	20	21	22	23	24
25	26	27	28	29	30	31

August						
S	M	T	W	T	F	S
1	2	3	4	5	6	7
8	9	10	11	12	13	14
15	16	17	18	19	20	21
22	23	24	25	26	27	28
29	30	31				

September						
S	M	T	W	T	F	S
			1	2	3	4
5	6	7	8	9	10	11
12	13	14	15	16	17	18
19	20	21	22	23	24	25
26	27	28	29	30		

October						
S	M	T	W	T	F	S
					1	2
3	4	5	6	7	8	9
10	11	12	13	14	15	16
17	18	19	20	21	22	23
24	25	26	27	28	29	30
31						

November						
S	M	T	W	T	F	S
	1	2	3	4	5	6
7	8	9	10	11	12	13
14	15	16	17	18	19	20
21	22	23	24	25	26	27
28	29	30				

How many months and days is it from July 23 to the:

a 28th of September? ____ months ____ days

b 9th of October? ____ months ____ days

c 29th of November? ____ months ____ days

❸ Use the split strategy to answer these sums.

a 43 + 32 = ____ b 53 + 26 = ____ c 64 + 12 = ____

31:3 1st, 2nd, 3rd, ____, ____, ____, ____

❶ Make a word from HOLIDAYS using:

- the 1st, 4th and 5th letters ____
- the 5th, 6th, 7th and 8th letters ____
- the 2nd, 3rd and 5th letters ____
- the 8th, 3rd, 4th and 5th letters ____

32:1 Double: 2 ☐ 4 ☐ 6 ☐ 7 ☐

❶ 2 × 5 = ____ 10 ÷ 2 = ____

2 × 8 = ____ 16 ÷ 2 = ____

2 × 4 = ____ 8 ÷ 2 = ____

2 × 7 = ____ 14 ÷ 2 = ____

❷ Double 1 ____ Double 5 ____

Double 10 ____ Double 3 ____

❸ This is half of my money.

How much money do I have altogether? ____

❹ Half of the cubes are hidden.

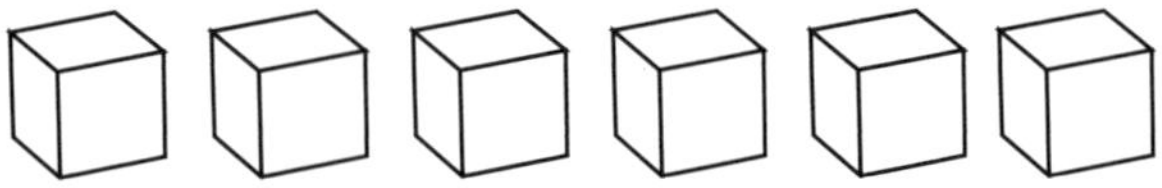

How many cubes are there altogether? ____

❺ There are 3 children.

How many ears are there? ____

____ groups of 2 = ____

❻ I can see 12 legs on a group of cows. How many cows are there?

____

❼ I can see 12 legs on a flock of birds. How many birds are there? ____

❽ Circle the shape that has parallel lines.

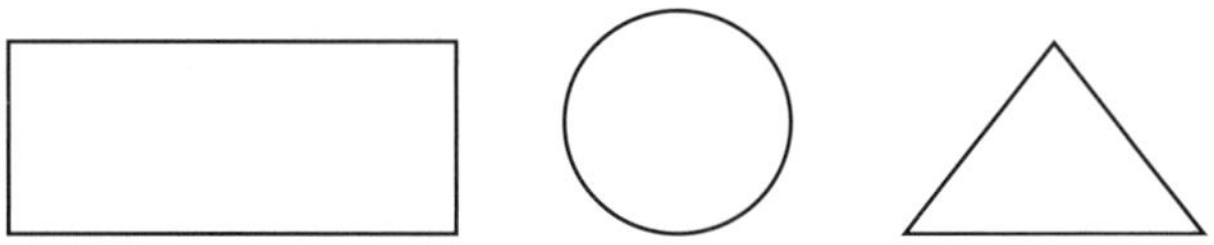

❾ Circle the correct word.

2 × **doubles** / **halves** a number.

❿ Cut this shape into halves. Colour one half.

⓫ Cut this shape into quarters. Colour one quarter.

⓬ Cut this shape into eighths. Colour one eighth.

⓭ There are 16 apples shared equally into 4 bags. How many are in each bag? ____

⓮ 12 blocks were used to build towers like this. How many towers could be built? ____

32:2

January, February, Autumn: March, April, May, Winter: June, July, August, Spring: September, October, November, Summer: December

1 **a** What is the date 2 weeks after August 4th? ________

b What is the date 2 weeks before August 30th? ________

c How many months are there in 2 years? ______

August						
S	M	T	W	T	F	S
1	2	3	4	5	6	7
8	9	10	11	12	13	14
15	16	17	18	19	20	21
22	23	24	25	26	27	28
29	30	31				

2 Draw lines to match each fraction picture with a word.

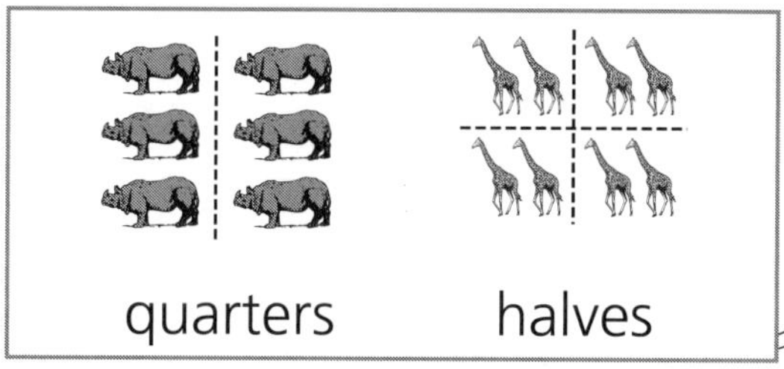

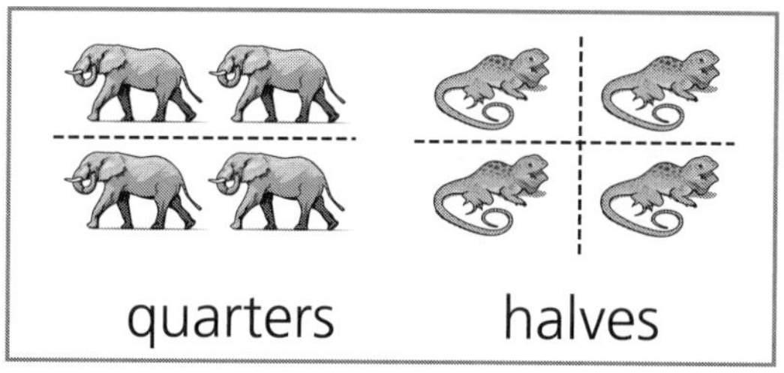

3 **a** I can see 16 legs on a herd of giraffes. How many giraffes are there? ______

b I can see 12 legs on a group of elephants. How many elephants are there? ______

4 I am standing at ⓧ. Where will I be if I move:

a 1 right then 2 forward? ________

b 5 forward then 2 left? ________

c 1 left then 4 forward? ________

d 1 right then 4 forward? ________

front

D		G		(teddy)
	F		H	
	C			(kite)
(drum)			E	
A		(toy)		
		ⓧ		B

32:3

Double: **1** ☐ **5** ☐ **10** ☐ **6** ☐

1 Complete each number web.

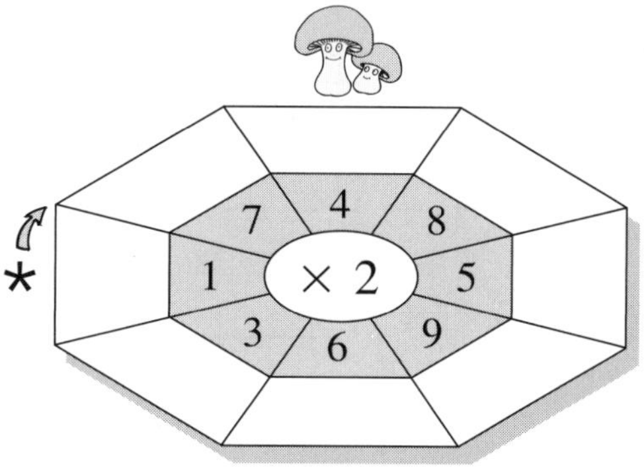

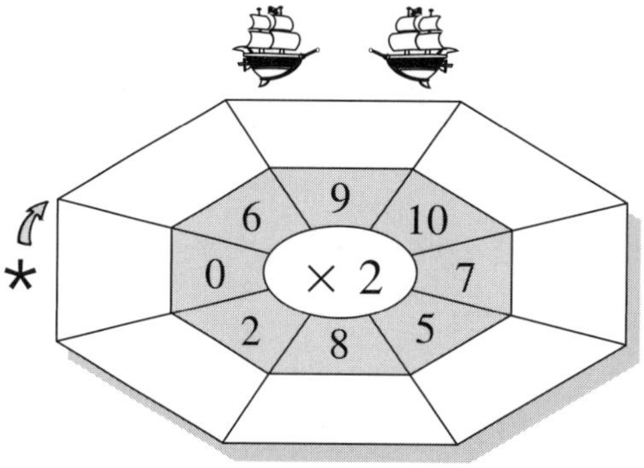

33:1 18, 16, 14, ____, ____, ____, ____, ____, ____

❶ Double 2 = ____

Double 3 = ____

Double 4 = ____

❷ This is half of my money.

How much money do I have? ____

❸ Halve 6. ____

Double your answer. ____

❹ Finish this turning pattern.

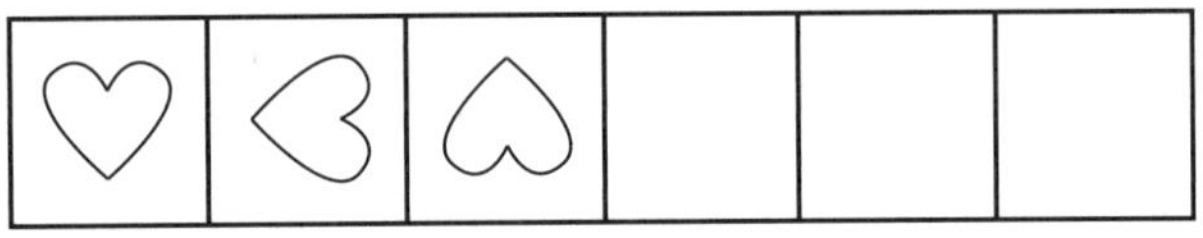

❺ Colour one eighth.

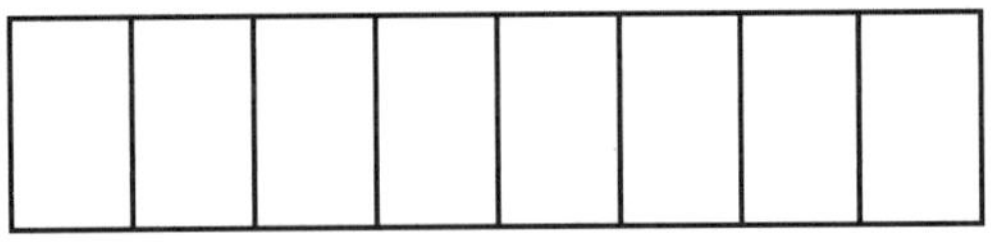

❻ Circle the correct word.
One **half / quarter** is shaded.

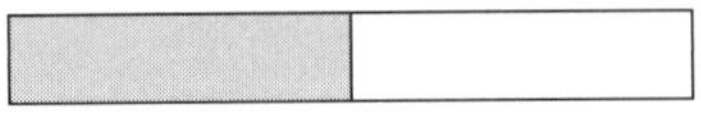

❼ 2 × 2 = ____ 4 ÷ 2 = ____

2 × 6 = ____ 12 ÷ 2 = ____

2 × 3 = ____ 6 ÷ 2 = ____

2 × 9 = ____ 18 ÷ 2 = ____

❽ 90, 80, 70, ____, ____, ____

2, 4, 6, ____, ____, ____

95, 90, 85, ____, ____, ____

13, 23, 33, ____, ____, ____

30, 35, 40, ____, ____, ____

❾ Half of the cubes are hidden.

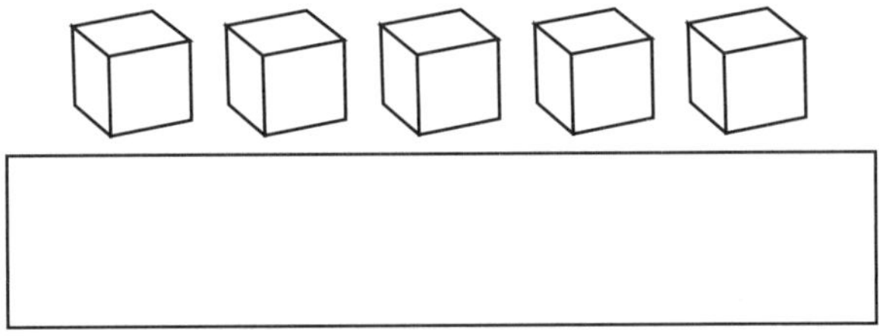

How many cubes are there altogether? ____

❿ Circle the correct answer.

÷ 2 **doubles / halves** a number.

⓫ Match the fraction to the part coloured.

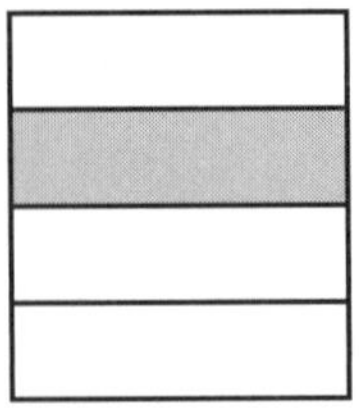

one quarter

one eighth

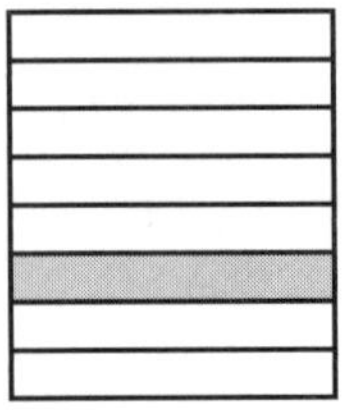

⓬ 5 + 5 ☐ 6 + 6 ☐ 7 + 7 ☐ 8 + 8 ☐ 9 + 9 ☐

 ISBN 978 0 6557 0882 7

33:2 31, 36, 41, ____, ____, ____, ____, ____, ____, ____

❶ Draw lines to cut these shapes into:

a halves **b** quarters **c** eighths

Colour one half. Colour one quarter. Colour one eighth.

❷ **a** What is the date 3 weeks after July 5th? ____________

b What is the date 3 weeks before July 29th? __________

c How many days are in July and August altogether? _____

July						
S	M	T	W	T	F	S
				1	2	3
4	5	6	7	8	9	10
11	12	13	14	15	16	17
18	19	20	21	22	23	24
25	26	27	28	29	30	31

❸ 9, 19, 29, ____, ____, ____, ____, ____, ____, ____, ____

209, 219, 229, ____, ____, ____, ____, ____, ____, ____

33:3

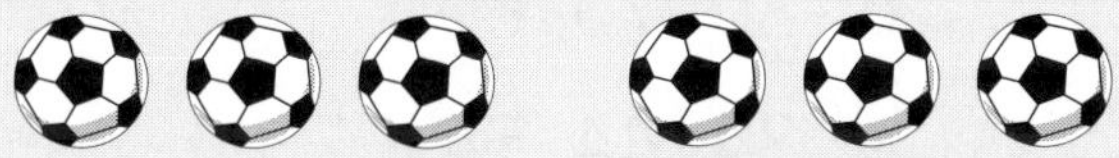

☐ **groups of** ☐ = ☐

❶ **a** Count backwards by twos from 100.

100, ____, ____, ____, ____, ____, ____

b Count backwards by tens from 100.

100, ____, ____, ____, ____, ____, ____

c Count backwards by fives from 100.

100, ____, ____, ____, ____, ____, ____

21	22	23	24	25	26	27	28	29	30
31	32	33	34	35	36	37	38	39	40
41	42	43	44	45	46	47	48	49	50
51	52	53	54	55	56	57	58	59	60
61	62	63	64	65	66	67	68	69	70
71	72	73	74	75	76	77	78	79	80
81	82	83	84	85	86	87	88	89	90
91	92	93	94	95	96	97	98	99	100

d Count backwards by twos from 79.

79, ____, ____, ____, ____, ____, ____, ____, ____

e Count backwards by tens from 89.

89, ____, ____, ____, ____, ____, ____, ____, ____

☐ groups of ten dogs = ☐

❶ Bridge to tens to find:

18 + 6 = _____ 27 + 4 = _____

❷ Use the best strategy to find:

7 + 8 _____

34 + 4 _____

19 – 3 _____

75 – 21 _____

❸ Use the jump strategy to find:

a 95 – 16 = ______

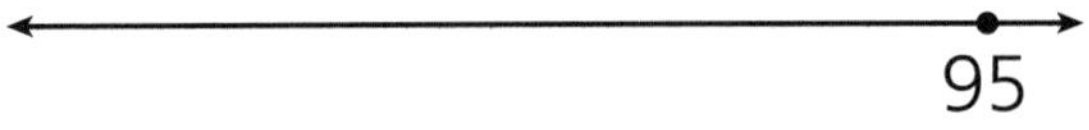

b 47 + 45 = ______

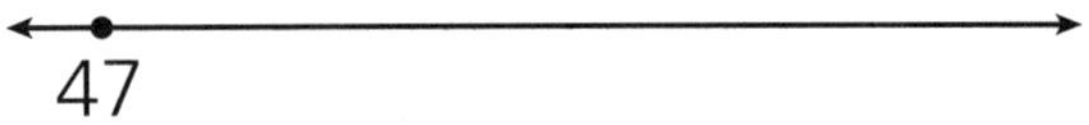

❹ Halve 8. _________

Double your answer. _______

❺ a 57 + 10 = _______ b 72 + 10 = _______ c 89 + 10 = _______

d 10 + 81 = _______ e 10 + 58 = _______ f 10 + 90 = _______

❻ Circle the two kangaroos above that show a turn.

❼ a Finish this turning pattern.

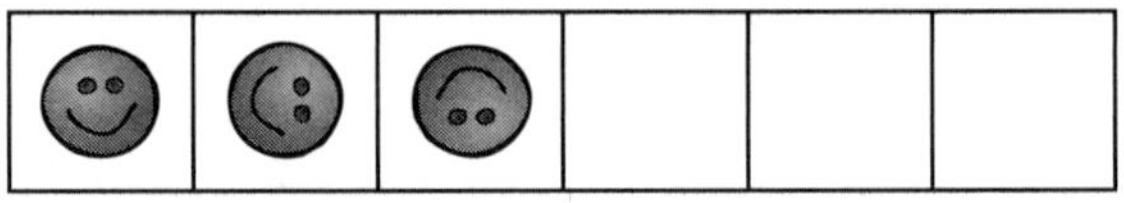

b Circle:
This pattern is made using **half / quarter** turns.

❽ a 75, 70, 65, _____, _____, _____

b 55, 50, 45, _____, _____, _____

c 42, 44, 46, _____, _____, _____

d 80, 70, 60, _____, _____, _____

e 34, 44, 54, _____, _____, _____

f 124, 134, 144, _____, _____

❾ This object is called

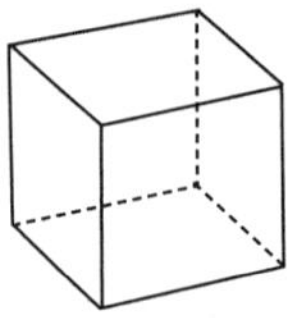

a _____________.

❿ What is the number before:

a 364? _____ b 720? _____

c 815? _____ d 698? _____

e 167? _____ f 466? _____

g 201? _____ h 300? _____

⓫ 5 + 3 ☐ 6 + 8 ☐ 4 + 7 ☐ 3 + 6 ☐ 5 + 7 ☐

34:2

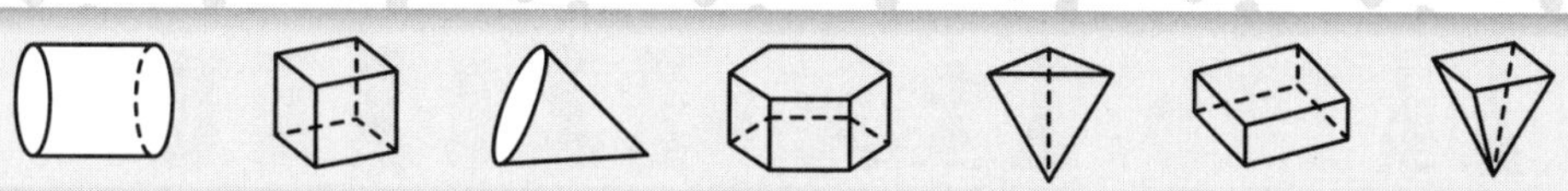

❶ Complete the table. (A face is a flat surface with straight sides.)

	Number of faces	Number of edges	Number of vertices	Number of curved surfaces	Number of flat surfaces
cylinder					
cube					

❷ 5, 15, 25, _____, _____, _____, _____, _____, _____, _____, _____

605, 615, 625, _____, _____, _____, _____, _____, _____, _____

7, 17, 27, _____, _____, _____, _____, _____, _____, _____, _____

207, 217, 227, _____, _____, _____, _____, _____, _____, _____

❸ **a** 46 + 17 = _____ **b** 52 – 37 = _____

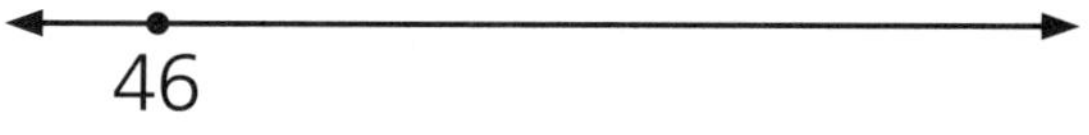

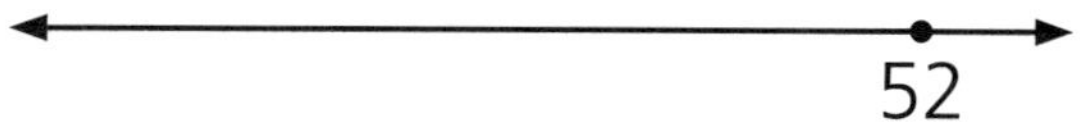

❹ 9 + 4 ☐ 9 + 6 ☐ 9 + 7 ☐ 9 + 5 ☐ 9 + 3 ☐

34:3

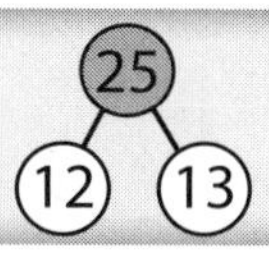

12 + 13 = 25 **25 – 12 = 13**

13 + 12 = _____ **25 – 13 = _____**

❶ Colour the shapes that have the same area as the square.

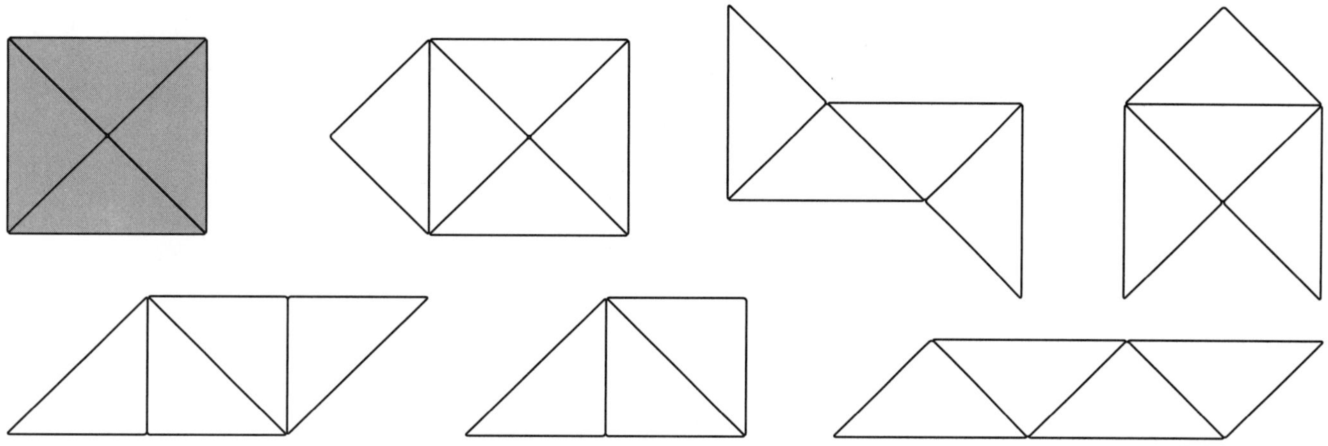

❶ Bridge to tens to find:

39 + 4 ____ 57 + 5 ____

68 + 5 ____ 27 + 4 ____

❷ Use the best strategy to find:

75 + 23 ____ 37 + 3 ____

8 + 7 ____ 61 + 31 ____

82 + 8 ____ 34 + 10 ____

❸ Use the number line to count on and find the difference between 27 and 44.

27 44

so 44 – 27 = ____

❹

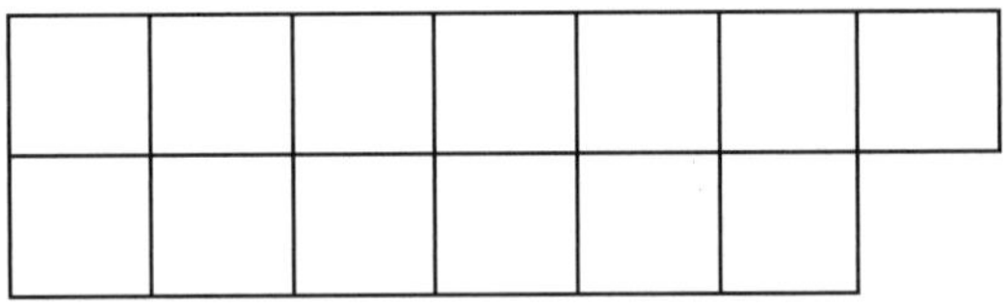

Write 3 different number sentences.

7 + ____ = 13

6 + ____ = 13

10 + ____ = 13

❺ 60, 58, 56, ____, ____, ____

❻ Use the pictures above to find:

a 3 + ____ = 5

b 2 + ____ = 3

c 6 + ____ = 11

❼

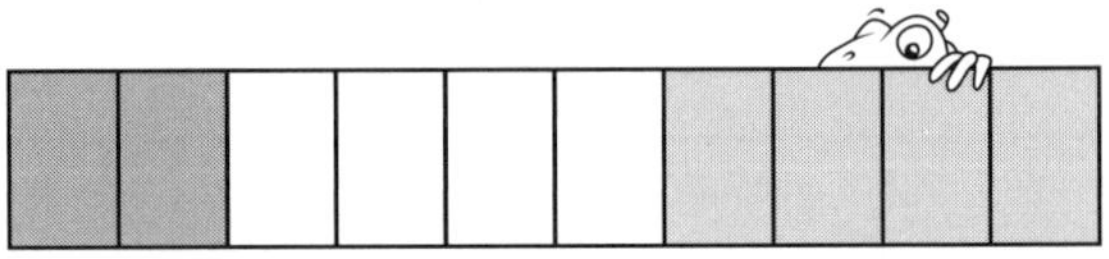

2 + 4 + ____ = 10

4 + 4 + ____ = 10

❽ 12 + ____ + 7 = 20

10 + 8 + ____ = 22

17 + ____ + 2 = 24

19 + ____ + 5 = 27

❾ 49 + 10 = ____ 81 – 10 = ____

23 + 20 = ____ 67 – 30 = ____

❿ How much money altogether?

a

____

b

____

⓫ 10 + 8 ☐ 10 + 2 ☐ 10 + 5 ☐ 7 + 10 ☐ 10 + 10 ☐

35:2

Name these 3D objects.

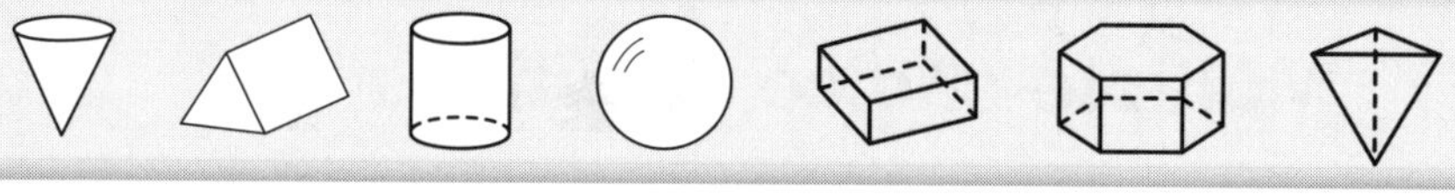

❶ Complete the table. (A face is a flat surface with straight sides.)

	Number of faces	Number of edges	Number of vertices	Number of curved surfaces	Number of flat surfaces
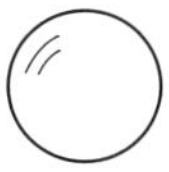					
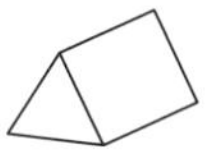					

❷ Use the split strategy to answer these sums:

a 53 + 45 = _____ **b** 62 + 24 = _____ **c** 41 + 52 = _____

❸ Use the jump strategy to find:

a 58 + 5 = ______

b 49 + 27 = ______

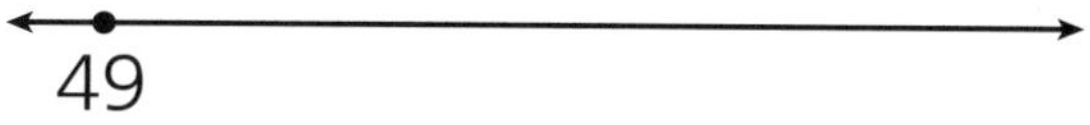

c 42 – 6 = ______

d 63 – 26 = ______

35:3

614, 624, 634, _____, _____, _____, _____, _____

❶

41	42	43	44	45	46	47	48	49	50
51	52	53	54	55	56	57	58	59	60
61	62	63	64	65	66	67	68	69	70
71	72	73	74	75	76	77	78	79	80
81	82	83	84	85	86	87	88	89	90
91	92	93	94	95	96	97	98	99	100

a Count backwards by tens starting from 100. Colour these red.

b Count backwards by fives starting from 100. Circle these as you go.

c Count by twos starting from 42. Shade these as you go.

 • *AUSTRALIAN SIGNPOST MATHS 2 MENTALS* • ISBN 978 0 6557 0882 7

Multiple-choice questions

Colour the oval next to the correct answer.

❶ What is the number that is one more than 40?

- 50
- 39
- 31
- 41

❷ Which of these shapes is a square?

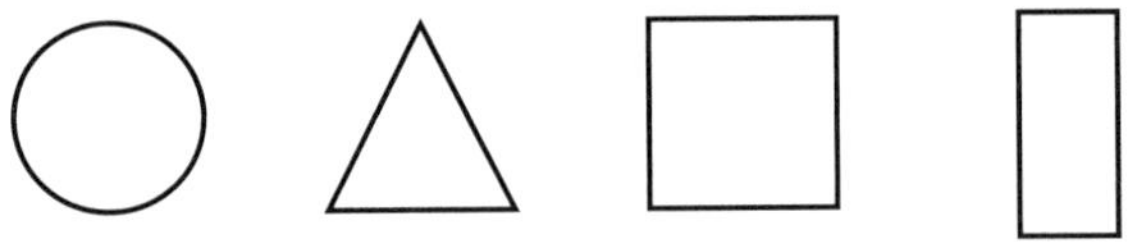

❸ Ice-blocks cost 50c each. How many can be bought for $1.00?

- 2
- 4
- 3
- 5

❹ These balloons show:

- 3 groups of 3
- 4 groups of 3
- 3 groups of 4
- 4 groups of 4

❺ 19 – 4 = ?

- 23
- 16
- 15
- 14

❻ Which of these is less than 10?

- 16
- 6
- 19
- 21

❼ The cloud is:

- below the bird
- above the bird
- to the right of the bird
- to the left of the bird

❽ Which number has a 2 in the tens place?

- 12
- 92
- 29
- 263

❾

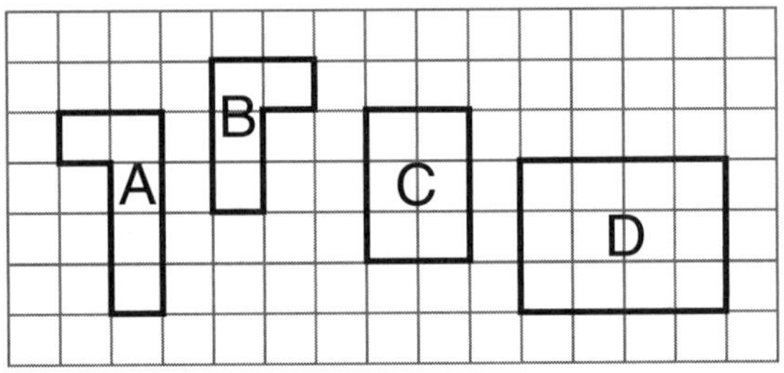

Which shape covers the largest area?

- A
- C
- B
- D

❿ Sue had 5 lollies. She was given 6 more.
How many lollies does she have altogether?

- 56
- 10
- 65
- 11

Problem-solving challenge

Use jottings and pictures, number lines or counters to solve these problems.

1. I took my wallet to the shops and spent 50c. I had 80c left. How much did I take to the shops?

   ____

2. 18 people are allowed in my pool at the same time. If there are 3 people in my pool, how many more are allowed to go in?

   ____

3. I did some jobs for my Nanna. I earned 20c for taking out the bins, 60c for folding the clothes and 80c for raking up the leaves. How much money did I earn?

   ____

4. **a** What number could I be? I am higher than 25 but lower than 30. The sum of my digits is 9.

   ____

   b What number am I? I am higher than 97. I am lower than 110. When my digits are added, the answer is 5.

   ____

5. **a** Start with the number 6. Double it. Add 4 to your answer. Halve that answer. What number do you finish with?

   ____

   b Start with the number 10. Add 2. Halve your answer then add 4. Double the last answer. What number do you finish with?

   ____

   c Write your own number question, like the two above.

   Start with the number ____________.

   ____

   ____

   ____

   ____

   ____

6. I am selling bracelets for 40 cents each. I need to earn $2 to buy a spinner. How many bracelets do I need to sell to make exactly $2? ____________

 • • ISBN 978 0 6557 0882 7

Problem-solving challenge

7 **a** I have used popsticks to make 5 separate triangles. How many pentagons could I make with the same number of popsticks?

b I have drawn a triangle, a hexagon and an octagon separately. How many sides did I draw?

Draw the three shapes below.

8 I read for 10 minutes on Monday, Tuesday and Wednesday. I read for 20 minutes on all the other days this week. For how long did I read this week?

9 There are 3 balls in our classroom. 2B has 2 more balls than our class has. 2A has 6 balls. How many balls are there altogether?

10 How many $5 notes do I need to make the same total as two $20 notes?

11 I bought a packet of biscuits. My sister ate 5, my Dad ate 3 and my Mum ate 4. There were 6 left. How many biscuits did I start with?

12 Sarah read 10 pages of her book every day for a week. How many pages did she read?

13 Mum bought two punnets of strawberries for Felicity, Lachlan and Jessica to share equally. Mum will eat the left over strawberries. If there are 23 strawberries altogether, how many strawberries will Mum eat?

 • *AUSTRALIAN SIGNPOST MATHS 2 MENTALS* • ISBN 978 0 6557 0882 7